Cost Accounting in Government

Managerial cost accounting is the financial and managerial tool that is used to estimate the organizational cost of products and services in business and government. In recent decades, cost accounting in the United States and other advanced industrial countries has been dominated by discussions of Activity-Based Costing, or ABC. While ABC can be shown to produce a more accurate estimate of cost than older and more basic types of cost accounting, ABC is not used extensively by many governments. We argue that this recent focus on ABC has stifled examination and discussion of how government cost accounting is being used and of how it could be used in practice. The study of cost accounting practice reveals an important and underexplored area of financial management in government.

Given the scandals that cost accounting estimates can create and that different types of cost accounting can create different estimates of cost, it may be reasonable to ask whether the cost accounting exercise is worth it? *Cost Accounting in Government: Theory and Applications* addresses these unusual and unusually important topics through a series of studies of different government cost accounting practices. The first section of the book presents two chapters on the history and the basic elements of cost accounting. The second section of the book provides further discussion and case studies of actual cost accounting practices in the main areas that cost accounting has been used in government: benchmarking the performance of government services, rate setting, grant overhead cost recovery, and cost management. The last two chapters discuss cost accounting practices in Europe and the future of cost accounting. These cases span local and federal governments and provide a much-needed context to the study of cost accounting in government.

Aimed at academics, researchers and policy makers in the fields of Accounting, Public Administration, and Government Studies, *Cost Accounting in Government: Theory and Applications* seeks to address the practical and theoretical gap in government cost accounting research with case studies of different public agencies that are using cost accounting for different purposes. The case studies illustrate that different purposes for cost accounting create unique and interesting cost accounting practices. The case studies provide useful examples of actual cost accounting systems that can inform both research and instruction.

Zachary Mohr is Assistant Professor in the Department of Political Science and Public Administration, the University of North Carolina at Charlotte, USA.

Routledge Studies in Accounting

For a full list of titles in this series, please visit www.routledge.com

Cost Accounting in Government
Theory and Applications

Edited by Zachary Mohr

Routledge
Taylor & Francis Group

LONDON AND NEW YORK

First published 2017 by Routledge

2 Park Square, Milton Park, Abingdon, Oxfordshire OX14 4RN
52 Vanderbilt Avenue, New York, NY 10017

Routledge is an imprint of the Taylor & Francis Group, an informa business

First issued in paperback 2019

Library of Congress Cataloging-in-Publication Data
Names: Mohr, Zachary, 1965– editor.
Title: Cost accounting in government : theory and applications /
   [edited by] Zachary Mohr.
Description: 1 Edition. | New York : Routledge, 2017. | Includes
   bibliographical references and index.
Identifiers: LCCN 2016052244 (print) | LCCN 2017012181 (ebook) |
   ISBN 9781315648897 (eBook) | ISBN 9781138123397
   (hardback : alk. paper)
Subjects: LCSH: Finance, Public—Accounting. | Cost accounting.
Classification: LCC HJ9750 (ebook) | LCC HJ9750 .C67 2017 (print) |
   DDC 657/.835042—dc23
LC record available at https://lccn.loc.gov/2016052244

ISBN: 978-1-138-12339-7 (hbk)
ISBN: 978-0-367-24293-0 (pbk)

Typeset in Sabon
by Apex CoVantage, LLC

Contents

8 **Extending the Application and Theory of Government
   Cost Accounting**   133
   ZACHARY T. MOHR

Figures

Tables

Abbreviations

A-122	OMB Cost Principles for Non-Profit Organizations
A-21	OMB Cost Principles for Educational Institutions
A-87	OMB Cost Principles for State, Local and Indian Tribal Governments
AAR	After-Action Review
ABC	Activity-Based Costing
ABM	Activity-Based Management
ACE	Analytic Cost Expert
AFAD	Allocate, Functionalize, Allocate, Distribute
AMCOS	Army Military and Civilian Costing System
AUB	Army Uniform Board
BEP	Bureau of Engraving and Printing
BOB	Bureau of the Budget
BSC	Balanced Scorecard
CAP	Cost Allocation Plan
CAPN	Cost Accounting Principles and Norms
CARB	Contract and Acquisition Review Board
CASB	Cost Accounting Standards Board
CBA	Cost–Benefit Analysis
CFR	Code of Federal Regulations
COCOPS	Coordinating for Cohesion in the Public Sector of the Future
ERP	Enterprise Resource Planning
FAA	Federal Aviation Administration
FAF	Financial Accounting Foundation
FASAB	Federal Accounting Standards Advisory Board
FORSCOM	Army Forces Command
FTE	Full-Time Equivalent Employee
FYDP	Five-Year Defense Plan
G1	United States Army Personnel
G4	United States Army Logistics Innovation Agency
G8	United States Army Office of Financial Management
GAAP	Generally Accepted Accounting Principles
GASB	Governmental Accounting Standards Board

GFOA	Government Finance Officers Association
GIS	Geographic Information Systems
IAS	International Accounting Standards
IASC	International Accounting Standards Committee
ICMA	International City/County Management Association
IT	Information Technology
MCS	Management Control Systems
MFOA	Municipal Finance Officers Association
NCGA	National Committee on Governmental Accounting
NPFM	New Public Financial Management
NPM	New Public Management
OMB	Office of Management and Budget
ONR	Office of Naval Research
PD	Production Department
PI	Principle Investigator
PM	Performance Measurement
PPBS	Program Planning Budgeting Systems
TCE	Transaction Cost Economics
TEL	Tax and Expenditure Limitation
TQM	Total Quality Management
UK	United Kingdom

Contributors

James W. Douglas, PhD, is a professor in the Department of Political Science & Public Administration at the University of North Carolina at Charlotte. His research specialization is in the area of public budgeting and finance, and his articles have appeared in journals such as *Public Administration Review*, the *Journal of Public Administration Research and Theory*, *Public Budgeting and Finance*, the *American Review of Public Administration*, the *American Journal of Political Science*, *Administration and Society*, and the *Journal of Policy Analysis and Management*.

Dale R. Geiger, PhD CMA CGFM, received his PhD from the Harvard Business School, where he did foundational work on the application of Activity-Based Costing (ABC) and cost accounting in the United States federal government. Dr. Geiger retired as a tenured professor at California State University and has also taught at George Washington University, the University of Southern California, the Naval Postgraduate School, and Georgetown University's Center for Professional Development. He has consulted for and done research on numerous federal agencies including the United States Navy, Air Force, Army, the General Accounting Office, the Internal Revenue service, and others. His research has appeared in *Accounting, Organizations, and Society* and *The Government Accountants Journal*. He is also the author of two books on cost accounting and cost management in the federal government: *Cost Management and Control in Government* and *Winning the Cost War: Applying Battlefield Management Doctrine to the Management of Government*.

Robert J. Eger III, PhD, is an associate professor in the Graduate School of Business and Public Policy at the Naval Postgraduate School. Dr. Eger is a leading voice in the United States on governmental accounting and financial management in government and not-for-profit organizations. He is the author of more than 30 peer-reviewed articles and book chapters. He is currently the editor in chief of the *Journal of Public and Nonprofit Affairs*. In 2011, he received the prestigious Chester A.

Newland Presidential Citation of Merit from the American Society for Public Administration.

Bruce D. McDonald III, PhD, is an assistant professor of public budgeting and finance in the Department of Public Administration at North Carolina State University. He is also an associate editor of the *Journal of Public and Nonprofit Affairs*. A graduate of Florida State University and the London School of Economics, his research has appeared in the *Annual Review of Political and Military Sociology*, the *Journal of Public Administration Research and Theory*, *Public Administration Review*, and the *Journal of Public and Nonprofit Affairs*, among others.

Zachary T. Mohr, PhD, is an assistant professor of political science and public administration at the University of North Carolina at Charlotte. He recently published two academic articles on local government cost accounting that appeared in *Public Budgeting and Finance* and *Public Administration Review*. He also has a forthcoming article on the relationship between cost accounting and transaction costs that will appear in *Public Administration Quarterly*. His government cost accounting work has been presented at academic conferences such as the American Accounting Association, the Association for Budget and Financial Management, the Association for Public Policy Analysis and Management, and others.

JoEllen Pope, CPA, is a PhD student at the University of North Carolina at Charlotte. Her research focuses on emergency management planning and on how government budgeting relates to planning activities. Prior to her PhD studies, Ms. Pope spent 20 years working as a CPA and owner of a public accounting firm. In addition, she served as a full-time firefighter for the City of Monroe, North Carolina. During her service, she participated as a member of the accreditation team responsible for authorship of the self-assessment manual.

Ringa Raudla, PhD, is a professor of public finance and governance at Ragnar Nurkse School of Innovation and Governance, Tallinn University of Technology, Estonia. She received her PhD in Economics from the University of Erfurt, Germany. Her research interests include fiscal governance, fiscal policy, public budgeting, institutional economics, public-sector accounting, and public management reforms. She has also worked as a consultant for various governmental and international organizations, including the Ministry of Finance of Estonia, the National Audit Office of Estonia, and the World Bank. Her recent publications include articles in *Public Administration Review*, *Governance*, the *Journal of Public Policy*, *Public Administration*, the *American Review of Public Administration*, the *International Review of Administrative Sciences*, *Europe-Asia Studies*, *Higher Education*, the *Accounting Auditing, & Accountability Journal*, and the *European Journal of Law and Economics*.

William C. Rivenbark, PhD, is a professor of public administration and government at the University of North Carolina. Dr. Rivenbark has been one of the leading figures for advancing the understanding of cost accounting's relationship to performance measurement and benchmarking in United States local governments through his work with the North Carolina Local Government Performance Management Project. He is the author of *Performance Budgeting for State and Local Government* (with Janet Kelly, M.E. Sharp, 2003). His work has also appeared in *Public Administration Review, Government Finance Review*, the *Journal of Government Financial Management*, the *Journal of Public Affairs Education*, the *Journal of Public Budgeting, Accounting & Financial Management, Popular Government, Public Administration Quarterly, Public Finance Review, Public Performance & Management Review, and State and Local Government Review*. He has also helped to develop the County and Municipal Fiscal Analysis tool, a web-based dashboard designed to help North Carolina local governments analyze their fiscal condition.

Preface

What person with any common sense would pay over $400 for a hammer? So why, ask critics, does the federal government? The reality is—despite media reports to the contrary—the federal government does not actually pay that much for hammers.

The $400 government hammer is an unfortunate problem for government financial management. Beyond the political sensitivity of the framing of the purchase, the real problem is the cost accounting that was done to derive the direct and indirect cost of the object or service. In the case of the hammer, a very large amount of indirect engineering costs was distributed down to a relatively limited quantity of direct costs, which gives the appearance of excessive expense and waste.

Given the scandals that cost accounting estimates can create and the recognition that different types of cost accounting can create different estimates of cost, it may be reasonable to ask whether the cost accounting exercise is worth it. The answer to this question is actually yes. For a variety of reasons, cost accounting is important in government and is not solely a tool that is used in private industry. For example, governments often have enterprises that they are trying to run like a business. To assure that they are not being subsidized indirectly by general tax sources, governments need to account for all of the direct and indirect costs of these enterprise services. Local governments are also asked to provide federal services in the United States to local populations because they are often the level of government that is in the best position to provide the services. However, and like the enterprise funds, cost accounting is needed so that the grant administration expense is not being subsidized by local tax revenues.

Unfortunately, there is not a lot of research about cost accounting. There is a little bit of research on why governments do cost accounting. There is less research on the problems or complications of cost accounting—even though we know from experience that cost accounting can encounter serious problems that can become very political. And we know almost nothing about why cost accounting systems differ and if those differences lead to different outcomes.

Because of these absences in the literature on government financial management and government accounting, we believe that the time is ripe for a book on cost accounting in government. We hope that it will create an interest to more thoroughly understand how cost accounting and costs, in a general sense, are being used in government and related organizations.

Already, there is more work being done on government cost accounting related topics by financial management scholars in Europe. This is likely a result of the global recession that started in 2008, but these commendable scholars are also likely responding to the vacuum that is so clearly present in the literature. This book focuses most specifically on cost accounting practices in the governments of the United States. This is primarily because there is even more of a dearth of literature on cost accounting practices in the United States. The penultimate chapter looks at cost accounting practices outside the United States and analyzes a unique survey of government employees on their cost accounting practices in European countries.

Overall, we hope that this book contributes to the still emerging literature on government cost accounting. Hopefully, it can serve as a foundation for financial management scholars on the topic in the United States and can serve as a bridge to the more developed literature in Europe and Australasian countries.

Introduction to Government Cost Accounting

Cost accounting is an important and recognized aspect of accounting, finance, and business management. Cost accounting is the measurement, analysis, and use of financial and nonfinancial information to determine the direct and indirect costs associated with the consumption of resources in an organization. Cost accounting for businesses is critical simply because businesses must price their products and services in a way that will recover all of the cost of the resources that were used to produce the service so that the business will stay solvent. For business cost accounting, this simple and profound raison d'être is enough to justify that every accounting student have at least one class, and sometimes two classes, in cost accounting. It is critical that accounting students are able to calculate the cost and profitability of services. Thus, cost accounting information is used by businesses to make decisions related to strategy, the budget, investments, production plans, pricing of services, and other critical business purposes.

It may seem unusual to start a book about government cost accounting by first talking about business cost accounting; however, the reason for business cost accounting must be acknowledged first and foremost so that we can realize that government does *not* need cost accounting for its survival. Profit is not the primary motive for government activities. Governments provide services where there is a market failure, either the under-provision of public goods or providing services that would result in a natural monopoly. In either case, a government that has the power to tax or effectively determine the market price does not need to turn a profit as its survival is not dependent upon an economic profit.

If not a profit motive, why does government do cost accounting? There are some general answers in the literature, and this book focuses on these activities because they illustrate the most important uses of cost accounting and the most important aspects that make cost accounting in government unique. Businesses do not often get grants from the federal government to give services away. Local governments in the United States do get grants, and they must account for their costs in providing these services in a way that can be ascertained and reimbursed so that the federal government does not unduly burden local governments. Local governments also provide services that they charge for such as transportation, water, sewer, gas, and electricity. These varied services would also benefit from good cost accounting so that they do not need to be subsidized by the general tax base. In sum, government services may be even more varied than private business and are, therefore, more likely to exhibit conceptually difficult variability when it comes to the cost accounting that is used.

This book is designed to start a discussion about government cost accounting. It provides a guide to the theory and research on its applications in government settings. As the literature on business accounting did in the 1970s, this research develops a descriptive theory of government cost accounting: when it is used, how it is used, and the unique aspects of government cost accounting. The following section describes the structure of the book proceeding from the general aspects, theory, and history of government cost accounting to the second part of the book, which further analyzes the primary purposes that have been described in the literature. The penultimate chapter looks at cost accounting outside the United States, and the final chapter discusses the potential for cost accounting in the future.

Structure of the Book

The first section of the book is made up of the first two chapters. This section provides background and foundations for understanding the cost accounting that is further elaborated on in the second section. These chapters cover the basics of what cost accounting is and the way that it has changed over time.

In the first chapter, Zachary Mohr provides a framework for understanding different cost accounting systems. The chapter presents the two archetypes of cost accounting for students to see how the different elements of cost accounting can lead to different estimates of cost. The chapter then proposes that in practice, these elements vary considerably based upon the purposes for which it is used and the forces that act upon it. It proposes that in practice the cost accounting that is used is a hybrid of the two textbook types of cost accounting. The theory of why this is appropriate for government cost accounting is then discussed with additional considerations that are important in different government contexts.

In the second chapter, William C. Rivenbark and Zachary Mohr contextualize cost accounting through different historical periods and note that it has changed considerably in its purposes over time. The use of cost accounting in government is not a new phenomenon. Fredrick Clow, the father of cost accounting in local government, published a manuscript in 1896 on the need for scholarly investigation into various aspects of municipal finance, which included a costing methodology for tracking efficiency trends over time and for making efficiency comparisons among multiple jurisdictions. Both scholars and practitioners have advocated the use of cost accounting in government on a period basis since that time, including Hebert Simon during the 1930s and Harry Hatry during the 1970s. The purpose of this chapter is to review the historical lineage of cost accounting in government to specifically identify why this tool has been promoted over the past 100-plus years from a theoretical and technical perspective. This chapter begins with a review of cost accounting in government beginning with the work of Clow (1896) before summarizing the theory that supports the management tool and the technical application of using resources consumed to calculate measures of efficiency. It concludes that the tool has changed significantly over time, but it remains a valuable tool for many purposes, including performance measurement and management.

The second section of the book covers chapters three through six. These four chapters look at the four primary applications or purposes for cost accounting in government: performance measurement, rate setting, grant overhead recovery, and cost management. The chapters generally discuss the important aspects of cost accounting for the application and provide a case study or description of how cost accounting has been used for this purpose.

In the third chapter, William C. Rivenbark notes the intrinsic value of cost accounting for benchmarking and performance measurement. Research in benchmarking has shown that the likelihood of local officials using performance indicators to make decisions actually increases when they engage in benchmarking, representing the process of comparing performance measures from one local government against performance measures from other local governments. This same research also found that local governments tend to rely more heavily on efficiency measures than effectiveness measures when making changes to service delivery. The underlying question, however, is how do local officials ensure an apple-to-apple comparison when comparing efficiency measures across multiple local governments given the complexities of how expenditures are accounted for from one organization to another? The purpose of this chapter is to explore the intrinsic value of cost accounting to increase the probability of accurately benchmarking service efficiency among multiple local governments. It begins with a literature review on benchmarking in local government before presenting the cost accounting methodology used by the North Carolina Benchmarking Project for calculating total resources consumed for a defined service area, which is the basis for producing an accurate and comparable cost per output measures. This chapter concludes by presenting several cases on how local governments participating in the North Carolina Benchmarking Project have used efficiency measures to advance the processes of service delivery.

In the fourth chapter, JoEllen Pope and Zachary Mohr discuss the important use of cost accounting for setting user fees and rates for government services. Increasingly, many government agencies rely on charging other agencies or outside organizations for a significant portion of their revenue. These agencies, in many cases, utilize cost accounting to establish the rates to be charged; however, not all agencies make use of cost accounting for rate setting. The purpose of this chapter is to examine the benefits of using cost accounting for rate setting and calculating user fees and identify issues that agencies might encounter. The chapter includes a special discussion of issues surrounding rate setting. The issues of cost accounting for rate setting and the trade-offs that must be made in this context are then discussed in the case of an internal charge between a city and an airport that became politically contested.

In the fifth chapter, Robert J. Eger and Bruce McDonald III explore the application of cost accounting principles and norms (CAPN) for state and local governments, nonprofits, and universities. The focus is on the budget, definition, disclosure statement, facilities and administrative costs, direct costs, and indirect costs contained within the grant. The objective of this chapter is to understand the application of CAPN to all financial aspects of the grant focusing on consistency in estimating, accumulating, and reporting costs while understanding the role of allowable and unallowable costs. In addition to the CAPN, this chapter will include the international accounting standard (IAS) 20, which is focused on accounting for government grants and disclosure of government assistance. IAS20 enriches the discussion of cost accounting for government grants by incorporating current aspects in the international accounting standards as they apply to grantee organizations in the United States.

In the sixth chapter, Dale R. Geiger explores the use of cost management tools in federal government agencies. As the fiscal resources of government become increasingly constrained, the management of operations becomes increasingly important in accomplishing the missions of government. Some federal organizations have demonstrated sustained capabilities in continuous improvement through several different forms of cost management and control: organization based, role based, and output based. The purpose of this chapter is to consider and contrast the cost accounting requirements of these successful innovators.

The third and final section of the book is to consider cost accounting beyond the current United States government context in which it has primarily been explored in the first six chapters of the book. The second-to-last chapter looks at cost accounting in European countries, and the final chapter looks at the prospects for cost accounting as a research subject into the future.

The seventh chapter by Ringa Raudla and James W. Douglas gives an overview of the use of cost accounting in the central governments of 19 European countries. Using data from a survey carried out within the framework of the largest comparative public management project undertaken in Europe so far, it provides a "cost accounting map" of the different countries, showing the variation in the intensity of the use of cost accounting within central government organizations. It explores the reasons that may explain the variation in the use of cost accounting between the European countries, including the role played by different administrative traditions, the influence of the paradigm of New Public Management, and the severity of fiscal stress. We also explore whether the use of cost accounting practices depends on the characteristics of the policy field and whether intercountry differences with regard to the utilization of cost-accounting are larger than the intracountry differences.

The final chapter by Zachary Mohr provides a summary of the purposes, problems, and the prospects for cost accounting in government. How each chapter addresses the linkage between the purpose and the corresponding problems and prospects is discussed. It provides avenues for the development of research on government cost accounting.

1 A Framework for Cost Accounting Systems in Government

Zachary T. Mohr

As a general concept, the need to understand and manage costs in government is a topic on which virtually no one is opposed, but the topic lacks extensive theoretical or empirical development. No one opposes the idea that the federal government should not spend thousands of dollars on a hammer, and no one opposes the idea that the local parks department uses the lowest cost provider to maintain its vehicle fleet. In difficult financial times, the most is expected of managers when it comes to service delivery cost, and to manage one's costs is a platitude that borders upon the obvious. Of course, these aspirations must meet the realities of actually determining the total cost of services in public organizations, forging agreement on which estimate of cost is appropriate, and then managing the costs. In spite of strong exhortations and the logic of cost efficiency and effectiveness, accounting for the full costs of public services, both direct and indirect costs, seems to be a challenge that has not been adequately addressed by public organizations, which tend toward less cost accounting than seems warranted based upon the purported benefits (Geiger, 2000, 2010; Mohr, 2015; Premchand, 2006).

The few researchers that have worked with cost accounting in government invoke a greater need for understanding it in this context, but they readily acknowledge that the understanding of government applications of cost accounting is "limited" (Rivenbark, 2000, 2005) and "underdeveloped" (Lienert, 2008; Robinson, 2007). A step toward developing knowledge of cost accounting in the government context is taken in this chapter by describing the two "textbook" types of cost accounting systems. A third type of cost accounting system, the hybrid cost accounting system, which exists between these two academic constructs (Goertz, 2006), is then described.

The need for cost accounting is tied to the observation that government agencies understate the cost of services when they do not include the cost of indirect resources in cost estimates (Geiger, 2000; Mohr, 2016), and the understated costs distort the rational allocation of public resources. Historically, cost accounting is used to allocate resources to the most cost efficient services, to recover revenue through grants and charges for services, and to evaluate performance (Mohr, 2015). It is often simplistically assumed that the best way to measure cost is to use the most advanced cost systems, such as activity-based costing (ABC), but this has to be weighed against the additional cost of measurement. More advanced cost accounting systems, like ABC, tend to provide more accurate estimates of the true cost of products and services (Cooper & Kaplan, 1988, 1992) and can be used for management and continuous improvement (Brimson, Antos, & Collins, 1999; Kehoe, 1995). For a variety of reasons, though, ABC may be inappropriate for general-purpose government use (Brown, Myring, & Gard, 1999; Collier, 2006; Flanagan & Britain, 2008; Flury & Schedler, 2006; Mullins & Zorn, 1999; Williams & Melhuish, 1999) and is not heavily used by cities in the United States[1] (Kennett, Durler, & Downs, 2007; William C. Rivenbark, 2005) or the federal government (Martin, 2005, 2007).

Developments in cost accounting since ABC, both scholarly and practical, provide a new foundation on which to understand different cost accounting systems and their managerial uses for government. By analyzing actual cost accounting systems that are being used by city and county governments, this chapter proposes that governments in the United States use hybrid cost accounting systems (Horngren, Datar, & Rajan, 2011) that combine features of traditional cost accounting and ABC. These developments in cost accounting provide a new basis upon which research about cost accounting systems in cities might proceed by providing a descriptive theory of cost accounting. This chapter reviews both traditional cost accounting, activity-based costing, and then proposes a hybrid form that is based on a review of actual systems in local governments. Attributes of each are compared to demonstrate the relevant differences and managerial uses for each type. It then reviews the main theories that have attempted to describe cost accounting in organizations with particular attention paid toward studies of government applications.

Types of Cost Accounting Systems in Government

In a historical analysis of cost accounting in the public sector, Rivenbark (2005) makes two important points about the general nature of cost accounting. The first is that cost accounting is to managerial accounting what fund accounting is to government financial accounting. In fact, managerial accounting is defined by the cost accounting exercise. Whether the cost accounting system is ABC or a more traditional cost accounting system, cost and managerial accounting must account for indirect costs (Mohr, 2016).

The other important point that Rivenbark makes for this analysis concerns a general disclaimer that needs to be made about cost accounting generally. Cost accounting has been implemented in different ways and is subject to various influences. This system has led to a nonstandard application of cost accounting. Where this chapter discusses traditional cost accounting, it is generally recognized that the "traditional" aspect is the standard textbook definition of a general cost accounting system and is a generalization for expository and academic purposes (Goertz, 2006). This in no way assumes that cost accounting systems are uniform. Research regarding cost accounting suggests that the government context is more varied than that in private organizations (Flury & Schedler, 2006), with the effect being that cost accounting systems in practice exhibit conceptually difficult variability (Rivenbark & Carter, 2000).[2]

The following discussions of cost accounting systems are an attempt to describe the two academic constructs of cost accounting and to provide a description of hybrid cost accounting, which can be seen in the systems used by local governments in the United States. It then compares the three types of cost accounting along the relevant dimensions discussed. The theory section of this chapter provides a further discussion of the factors that lead to differences in cost accounting and suggests why hybrid cost accounting may have developed in local government.

Traditional Cost Accounting

Traditional cost accounting has been likened to spreading overhead costs over the departments of an organization like peanut butter being spread over a piece of bread (Kehoe, 1995). This metaphor captures the essence of traditional cost accounting because it will generally smooth the costs of overhead across the service departments of an organization. The reason that it smooths the costs over the organization is that traditional cost accounting uses allocation bases that vaguely link products and services to overhead resource consumption. The general nature of the bases generally distributes overhead and may not direct it in the system to the parts of the organization that are actually using the majority of the overhead. This smoothing makes the managerial uses of traditional cost accounting information not particularly useful for management purposes such as controlling overhead resource consumption by the service departments.

The most common cost objective, or use, of traditional cost accounting is to allocate the cost of overhead to the service providing departments and programs for the purpose of grant and financial reporting compliance (Flury & Schedler, 2006; Rivenbark, 2005). If the overhead costs were to be left out, this would significantly understate the true cost of providing that service and grant-funded activities may not be completely reimbursed, assuming, of course, that the grant allows the allocation of indirect or overhead costs. When overhead is not allowed by granting agencies, the local government must support the overhead costs from its own resources. When grants do allow for the provision of the capture of overhead and indirect costs, governments that do not allocate overhead costs to the grants give up resources that could be used to increase the welfare of local citizens.[3] Traditional cost accounting systems could also be used to include some measure of overhead cost for pricing services that would be provided by a user charge. However, this method of pricing goods and services was inaccurate as has been pointed out by proponents of ABC. Traditional ways of allocating indirect costs in traditional cost accounting are to use either the direct or the step-down method, where overhead costs are allocated down to service departments in either one or two steps (Finkler, Purtell, Calabrese, & Smith, 2012).

An example of the traditional cost accounting system for the services of one department can be found in the hypothetical example of the City of Frugal[4] (Figure 1.1). The budget for the departments of Frugal is presented first. The first thing to notice with the traditional cost accounting plan is the allocation bases that will be used to distribute the costs to the departments. The

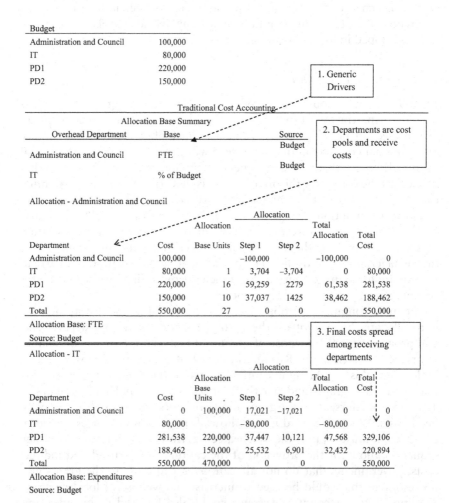

Figure 1.1 Traditional Cost Accounting System Example

allocation bases are general and ambiguously linked to overhead resource consumption, such as the use of Full-Time Equivalent (FTE) Employees or department's expenditures from the budget to distribute the cost (see the following example). As was noted previously, the effect of these general cost drivers is to spread the cost of the overhead departments between the receiving departments with little recognition of actual resource use and less ability to show managers how to control overhead costs.

In the traditional cost accounting system, it may *not* be necessary to drive the cost down to products and services as is done with ABC.[5] The receiving cost centers are departments or general categories of spending such as a grant service. Not only are the receiving departments general but so are the overhead cost pools. In this example, there are two cost pools that will be distributed to two department cost centers. The Administration and Council cost center has multiple activities that it performs, but all of the cost associated with all of these different activities are distributed in an equivalent way based on the number of employees. The Information Technology (IT) department also is a general cost pool with a general driver, which leads to ambiguous allocation of costs.

The costs of the administrative departments are allocated using the double-step-down method. It first takes the cost of the cost pool and allocates those costs on the basis of the driver to both overhead and service departments.[6] In the second allocation, the allocated costs from the first step down that were distributed to other overhead departments are then allocated based upon the remaining drivers to the service departments. The final cost of service departments is shown after the allocation for IT, where the Production Department 1 (PD1) accounts for $329,106 of the $550,000 cost and the Production Department 2 (PD2) accounts for $220,894 of the $550,000. The costs of the overhead departments have been spread across the service departments in a way that roughly corresponds with each department's share of the budget relative to the other service department. While the traditional cost accounting system can distribute the costs to the service department, these costs may not reflect the actual consumption of overhead resources.

Activity-Based Costing

Traditional cost accounting benefits from over a century of research and development in both municipal and federal government (Kraines, 1970; Rivenbark, 2005; Rubin, 1993). The relatively more recent activity-based costing (ABC) was proposed by Cooper and Kaplan (Cooper & Kaplan, 1988, 1992; Kaplan, 1988; Kaplan & Cooper, 1998) and comes from the critique that traditional cost systems were failing to provide the meaningful information on the costs of individual products and services needed for businesses to compete in a highly competitive, global environment (Johnson & Kaplan, 1987). Instead of just passing down overhead costs to cost centers such as departments or programs, the cost objects of ABC are the individual products and services that the business makes and sells. These ideas were applied to governments that also had their own pressures to be more efficient and make difficult choices among services in the 1990s (Brimson et al., 1999; Kehoe, 1995; Weiss, 1997). Because of its more recent prominence, somewhat more is known about actual applications of ABC in modern governments than traditional cost accounting, but the knowledge and the applications of ABC have not led to a standard ABC development.[7] Due to this lack of development in the literature on a standard process for local governments to develop an ABC system, the general four-step process of ABC (Gosselin, 1997) is first discussed, and then the key elements of ABC are differentiated for contrast with traditional cost accounting.

The first step to any ABC system is "to identify the activities being performed by the organization's support resources" (Kaplan & Atkinson, 1998, p. 97). Within the ABC framework, the cost center is no longer the central focus of the analysis, and the central focus becomes the support resources that may come from either overhead cost centers or from the indirect costs within the service centers to provide a good or service. This distinction is important because a service center may provide many services and have many resources. In the ABC framework, the goal is to align the resources consumed to the production of products and services. This necessitates that the first step is to track the activities of support and service centers, which will eventually be used to determine all of the costs that go into each and every activity.

In the second stage of the ABC system, managers or accountants trace the costs of indirect costs to products or services by determining the "activity cost driver" or "cost driver." The cost driver is some quantifiable measure that can connect indirect costs to individual products or services through a "cause and effect relationship." ABC provides the mechanism to establish a causal relationship between common costs that must be ignored by traditional cost systems because managers are not provided the information they need to understand and control their usage of common costs (Kaplan & Atkinson, 1998, p. 99). Research in actual government settings provides some guide to the type of driver required (Geiger, 1999), but in general the driver should be specific to establish the cause-and-effect relationship between indirect resources actually used and resources accounted for in the cost attribution.

In the third stage of ABC, everything is put together to determine the full cost of doing an activity such as production or providing a service. The ABC designer links the indirect costs to the cost drivers identified and the direct costs of service to determine the actual cost of production or service. The key is that every cost is logically connected to the output. The estimate obtained is usually much more accurate because it is not based upon arbitrary allocation or overly generalized bases. It is in this stage that the true costs of activities are revealed. The purpose of ABC is to ultimately give managers the information that they need to determine which products, services, customers, and processes add value to the mission of the organization. Services that do not add value should be redesigned or eliminated to increase the value of the organization. In the case of one nonprofit healthcare clinic, new information from ABC about the cost of services revealed that one of its dialysis treatments that the clinic thought was profitable was actually being subsidized by another dialysis treatment that was previously thought to be unprofitable (Kaplan & Atkinson, 1998). Once the true costs of services were known it was easy to determine that the customers that could receive the second type of treatment should receive it. With their old cost accounting system, the managers had been funneling their patients into an overly costly and unprofitable service. In this case, the customer and the clinic can be made better off by the increased awareness of the true cost of services.

The fourth and final stage is the active management of an organization's costs based upon the information obtained from an ABC process. This is also known as Activity-Based Cost Management or just Activity-Based Management (ABM). ABM generally requires some sort of process reengineering, total quality management, cost-of-quality analysis, continuous improvement, process modeling and simulation, value analysis, benchmarking, and others (Kehoe, 1995). In any case, information being used extensively in the management of an organization pushes an organization beyond activity based cost accounting and into ABM.

While the details of ABC such as cost drivers, attribution, and indirect costs are obviously different from traditional cost accounting, the major difference is the purpose of the system. Activity-based costing provides government managers and controllers a cost accounting technique that is specific enough to track the indirect resource consumption of individual products and services and then allows these costs to be managed. This focus on individual products and services and the specific cost drivers that it requires are the biggest differences between traditional cost accounting and ABC. Another important difference is that ABC promotes a hierarchy of costs that are traceable and avoidable. This hierarchy of cost concept is important to allow meaningful comparisons of the contribution margin of the various activities. While contribution margin analysis is primarily beneficial for services and products that are produced in a manufacturing environment, the same sort of marginal analysis may be important for setting optimal levels of service from a policy-theoretic framework as well.

For purposes such as grant reimbursement, traditional cost accounting may give an acceptable estimate of cost, but it usually does not give extremely accurate information for individual products or services. The original purpose of ABC was to provide managers with the information that they needed to have more profitable products and services and improve their processes (Kaplan & Cooper, 1998). While financial profitability is not a concern for government as much as it is with business (Flury & Schedler, 2006; Mullins & Zorn, 1999), the use of more specific cost drivers to increase knowledge of processes, drive organizational learning, and increase efficiency is a concern for government managers (Brimson et al., 1999; Kehoe, 1995; Weiss, 1997), especially in times of fiscal scarcity (Geiger, 2010). These arguments for the utility of ABC often contrast with its extremely low levels of usage in public organizations such as cities (Kennett et al., 2007).

The hypothetical example of Frugal can be used to show how an ABC system specifically attributes the costs of indirect resources to develop a more accurate cost for products and services. The following example starts with the same small community, Frugal, with two overhead departments: Administration and Council and the IT department (See Figure 1.2). After doing an activity analysis, it is found that the Administration and Council cost pool are doing two distinct activities. The IT department is found to be doing primarily one activity, which is servicing the computers of the departments. For brevity, the example assumes that the service departments, PD1 and PD2, each do one activity. In a real example, departments do multiple activities, and using ABC the city could trace the cost down to the activity level in these departments using the method described.

Once the activity analysis is completed, the government then figures out cost drivers that are logically linked to the indirect resource usage. The first indirect resource is general administration, and it is found that the general nature of the administrative functions performed can only be based on the time the administrative officers of the city spent with the activities of the Council, IT, and the service departments. The Administration department begins tracking its time in the payroll system as a realistic way of basing the costs of administration. Of the proportion of the Council's time to be allocated, it is thought fair to distribute those costs based upon the number of agenda items that the council has to review. Also, the cost driver for IT is found to be the number of computers in each department, as that is the primary activity with which the department is concerned. The key to activity based cost drivers is that they unambiguously link the consumption of overhead costs with the direct costs of services.

An important difference between the ABC system of cost accounting and the traditional cost accounting system is the recognition that some costs may not be appropriate to distribute to the lower levels of service providing departments, because some of those costs are necessary to sustain the organization. In this case, only half of the Council's cost is attributed to the service departments because only half of the Council's time has been found to be related to actual departmental issues. A large portion of the time is related to general organizational maintenance activities such as interacting with citizens. This hierarchy of costs concept is as applicable at the departmental level that is being developed here and the within-department level when specific activities have costs that only apply to the batch and product-sustaining level (Kaplan & Atkinson, 1998). In both ABC and economic theory, the only costs that should be passed to the lower level activities are

Overhead Department	Driver Summary Drivers	Source
Administration	Time	Payroll System
Council	50% Self & 50% Agenda Items	Council Minutes
IT	Computers	IT Records

1. Specific cost drivers

2. Hierarchy of cost

Activity - Administration

Activity	Cost	Driver units	Allocation Step 1	Step 2	Total Allocation	Total Cost
Administration	80,000		−80,000		−80,000	0
Legislature	20,000	384	8,000	−8,000	0	20,000
IT	80,000	384	8,000	889	8,889	88,889
PD1 Activity/Service	220,000	1,728	36,000	4,000	40,000	260,000
PD2 Activity/Service	150,000	1,344	28,000	3,111	31,111	181,111
Total	550,000	3,840	0	0	0	550,000

Driver: Administrative Time
Source: Payroll System

3. Activities are cost pools and activities receive cost

Activity - Council

Activity	Cost	Driver units	Allocation Step 1	Step 2	Total Allocation	Total Cost
Administration	0	1	357	−357	0	0
Legislature	20,000		−10,000		−10,000	10,000
IT	88,889	2	714	26	741	89,630
PD1 Activity/Service	260,000	5	1,786	66	1,852	261,852
PD2 Activity/Service	181,111	20	7,143	265	7,407	188,519
Total	550,000	28	0	0	0	550000

Driver: Agenda Items
Source: Council Minutes
Note: 50% of Legislative cost is allocated, other 50% allocated to self

Acitivity – IT

Activity	Cost	Driver units	Allocation Step 1	Step 2	Total Allocation	Total Cost
Administration	0	4	21,089	−21,089	0	0
Legislature	10,000	1	5,272	−5,272	0	10,000
IT	89,630		−89,630		−89,630	0
PD1 Activity/Service	261,852	2	10,545	4,394	14,938	276,790
PD2 Activity/Service	188,519	10	52,723	21,968	74,691	263,210
Total	550,000	17	0	0	0	550,000

Driver: Agenda Items & Council Minutes

4. Final costs related to resource consumption

Figure 1.2 Activity-Based Costing System Example

those that are both traceable and avoidable, although these concepts are rarely empirically observed (for an exception see Anderson & Sedatole, 2012).

Once the activities of the indirect resource departments are attributed with clear and specific drivers to the activities performed by the organization, the indirect resources can be attributed to the products and services of the organization. As in the traditional cost accounting example, the double-step-down methodology is used. In this example, Administration has to be distributed before the Council and then the IT department. After all the service departments have attributed their indirect resources to the service departments, it is apparent that the PD2 consumes much more indirect resources than PD1. After the allocations from the three overhead cost pools, the total direct and indirect cost of providing the PD2 service is almost as much as the cost of providing the PD1 service, even though the direct cost of the PD1 service is $80,000 greater than the cost of the PD2 service, according to the budget. This example shows how ABC develops a generally better estimate of actual resource usage. The final cost also shows that some overhead resource costs such as Council expense are more general organization related than service related. Distributing these costs fully, or a full attribution, as is done with the traditional cost accounting system may overstate the true cost of services.

Hybrid Cost Systems: Between Traditional Cost Accounting and ABC System

The preceding analysis of traditional cost accounting systems and ABC systems is intended to contrast the two ends of the spectrum that are noted in the literature. The purpose of this chapter is to suggest and show that there is an intermediate position (and perhaps multiple positions) between the two poles for cost accounting in practice. This system represents a hybrid between the traditional cost system and the ABC system and is conceptually similar to the "hybrid system" of the accounting literature (Horngren et al., 2011). The "hybrid" system contains a mixture of both traditional and activity-based cost elements.

The example that Horngren et al. give of the hybrid system is specialized shoe manufacturing. These specialized shoe systems that can be found on the Internet and at specialized shops for making custom, brand name shoes have both activity specific cost drivers such as the level of customization, but they also have more general cost drivers such as the general cost of the base shoe. While an ABC system would map the activities for each individual shoe and give it a price, the level of individual customization makes this nearly impossible. Instead, the shoe manufacturer relies on a general cost and then builds on it using specific cost drivers such as separate colors, materials, or orthotic support. The hybrid cost system balances the cost of the system with the benefit by providing a mix of general and specific cost drivers.

The same mentality of balance between the cost and benefit of the system can be readily seen when one identifies formal cost plans in local governments. In December 2011, the cost plans of all cities with a population greater than 100,000 were requested. From the 272 cities in the sample, cost plans from 30 cities were received, which included 134 separate documents.

This large number is because several cities have multiple cost plans, and a couple of cities sent several years of cost accounting documents and source material. Upon reviewing and coding the 2011 plans for type and number of cost drivers for common overhead and production activities, it became apparent that the plans contain a mix of specific and generic cost drivers but only rarely have a hierarchy of costs. Representative examples of these plans can be found on the City of Houston and the City-County website of Nashville-Davidson County.[8] These plans are developed under the pressures that governments face: the need to be efficient even with the cost of making and maintaining their cost plans. The variety of development within the different types of cost plans indicates that the cost systems of local governments are a hybrid type of cost accounting that exhibit characteristics of both traditional and ABC systems.

The hybrid cost system exhibits varied development of the critical dimensions of difference between traditional and activity-based cost systems. For example, the hybrid system has a mix of general and specific cost drivers. While the traditional cost system uses basic cost drivers to roughly allocate the indirect resources down to service providing departments, the hybrid system uses some generic cost drivers and some specific drivers. For example, the City of Houston 2010 Full Cost Plan shows that cost drivers for the human resource department included full-time employees, classified full-time employees, selections, and number of employees trained (Maximus, 2009). Half of the human resources cost drivers are specific, but this percentage of general, and specific drivers can vary widely from department to department. This allows the hybrid system to have some claim to an unambiguous link to overhead resource consumption but, perhaps, not completely or in all departments or services. The number and type of cost drivers are critical to the development of the hybrid cost plan and those that generally have more specific cost drivers are more similar to ABC and those with fewer and basic cost drivers more like the traditional cost accounting systems.

Hybrid cost systems may also not have a hierarchy of costs or distribute the indirect resources of activities all the way down to products or services. The following example (Figure 1.3) is an illustration of the Frugal example using a hybrid system. First, it has a mix of general and specific cost drivers. Rather than keeping track of all the time spent on department business, the administration might logically conclude that it would be more cost effective to simply use the number of FTE in each department as a general cost base. Second, the hybrid system may not have a hierarchy of costs for the council. All of the cost of the council is distributed down to the service departments. Next, the indirect or overhead resources distributed by the hybrid system may be sent to either products and services or general departments. Finally, the cost of indirect resources is not spread evenly over the organization like the traditional cost accounting system, but it also is not as unambiguous as the ABC system. Generally, the hybrid system with mostly specific cost drivers develops a better estimate than traditional cost systems but not quite as specific as ABC.

Having specific drivers not only increases the accuracy of the cost information about true cost of service, but it also increases the value of the information relative to traditional cost accounting. If the cost drivers vary from period to period, it will facilitate cost management and organizational learning (Geiger, 2010). Organizational leaders can use periodic hybrid cost data to do variance analysis of indirect resource consumption, streamline processes, and make better product or service allocation decisions. However,

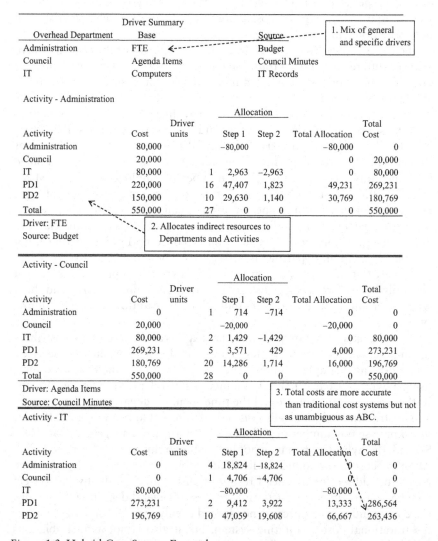

Driver Summary

Overhead Department	Base	Source
Administration	FTE	Budget
Council	Agenda Items	Council Minutes
IT	Computers	IT Records

1. Mix of general and specific drivers

Activity - Administration

Activity	Cost	Driver units	Allocation Step 1	Step 2	Total Allocation	Total Cost
Administration	80,000		−80,000		−80,000	0
Council	20,000				0	20,000
IT	80,000	1	2,963	−2,963	0	80,000
PD1	220,000	16	47,407	1,823	49,231	269,231
PD2	150,000	10	29,630	1,140	30,769	180,769
Total	550,000	27	0	0	0	550,000

Driver: FTE
Source: Budget

2. Allocates indirect resources to Departments and Activities

Activity - Council

Activity	Cost	Driver units	Allocation Step 1	Step 2	Total Allocation	Total Cost
Administration	0	1	714	−714	0	0
Council	20,000		−20,000		−20,000	0
IT	80,000	2	1,429	−1,429	0	80,000
PD1	269,231	5	3,571	429	4,000	273,231
PD2	180,769	20	14,286	1,714	16,000	196,769
Total	550,000	28	0	0	0	550,000

Driver: Agenda Items
Source: Council Minutes

3. Total costs are more accurate than traditional cost systems but not as unambiguous as ABC.

Activity - IT

Activity	Cost	Driver units	Allocation Step 1	Step 2	Total Allocation	Total Cost
Administration	0	4	18,824	−18,824	0	0
Council	0	1	4,706	−4,706	0	0
IT	80,000		−80,000		−80,000	0
PD1	273,231	2	9,412	3,922	13,333	286,564
PD2	196,769	10	47,059	19,608	66,667	263,436

Figure 1.3 Hybrid Cost System Example

if it is distributed to a general cost pool or using a generic allocation base, the uses for the cost information may be more limited. The use of generic cost drivers does not allow extensive management of indirect resource consumption because the generic cost driver is not linked unambiguously to the indirect resource and often does not change enough to meaningfully be used to guide decisions about resource usage.

Comparison of the Three Systems

Table 1.1 describes key features of the three types of systems discussed. The key dimensions focus the point of discussion on the reasons for the cost system. Cost and benefit are standard considerations for any organization developing a cost system, but government systems may have multiple purposes for which they are trying to maximize the benefit to the organizations. Many cities have multiple cost accounting plans. The reason for this was that some cities had additional cost plans in addition to the cost plan that meets the specific requirement of 2 CFR Part 225 (formerly A-87)

Table 1.1 Key Attributes of Different Cost Systems

Cost System Attributes	Traditional Cost Accounting Systems	Hybrid Cost Accounting Systems	ABC Systems
Cost objective	Department/ Program	Some department and some programs/ activities	Mostly specific programs and activities
Indirect Costs	Only overhead departments	All overhead and some service departments	All overhead and departments with multiple activities
Driver quality	Generic	Specific and generic	Specific
Driver quantity	Few	Intermediate	Multiple based upon number of activities
Hierarchy or cost avoidability	No hierarchy, full costs or full absorption costing	Some hierarchy and avoidability considered	Explicit hierarchy of costs (traceable and avoidable)
Reason for the system	Compliance and reporting; to provide information on the average cost of services	Rate setting, general cost management such as variance analysis for specific areas	Continuous improvement; activity based management, managed competition and contracting
Cost accuracy & Benefits	Good	Better than traditional	Best
Cost of the cost accounting	Some	More than traditional	Most

for federal grant overhead costs. Overall, this multiplication of the systems shows that cities in federal systems must respond to multiple factors that promote a cost accounting that responds to the dictum of "different costs for different purposes" (Horngren et al., 2011) and that cost accounting that is practiced by public organizations is neither traditional or ABC. In both general cost plans and those specifically designed for federal grant compliance, the cost plans have a mix of the number, type, and cost centers in the plans, which make all of the plans more similar to the hybrid system previously discussed.

The key attributes of the cost systems in Table 1.1 conceptualizes hybrid cost accounting as somewhere between traditional and activity-based cost accounting. As such, the relevant dimensions are usually in-between the traditional and ABC systems. For example, the traditional cost accounting is conceptualized as very basic, and the only relevant cost centers that have resources allocated down to production centers are the general overhead departments like facilities and administration. In contrast, the ABC system has cost centers in both overhead departments and in departments that have multiple activities that share some departmental resources. Between these extremes is the hybrid system that has overhead costs allocated and in some specific instances has shared departmental overhead split down to some of the activities.

As was previously discussed, hybrid cost accounting systems also have a mix of specific and generic cost drivers, and hybrid cost accounting has multiple cost drivers in some departments based upon the specific activity analysis for the department or cost center. Finally, the hybrid system may have a hierarchy of cost in some cost centers and not others. This leads to a mix of avoidable and nonavoidable costs that require professional evaluation and judgment to use for managerial decisions.

This variation is hypothesized to be related to the type of use of the cost accounting and factors within the city that may influence the cost accounting. For example, the traditional cost system may only be used for basic purposes like crude overhead cost recovery for grants. The ABC system is a very intensive user of information and technology resources (Kaplan & Anderson, 2007) and would primarily be used in government for continuous improvement of processes and activity-based management to reduce the costs of individual products and services, potentially by indicating activities and services that could be beneficially contracted to an outside service provider. Between these different systems is the hybrid system that has uses that are more interrelated and perhaps achieve multiple purposes. The hybrid system is generally best suited for rate setting where it minimizes the cost of information needed by the system and the cost of errors from the system but may also be suitable for grant overhead cost recovery. Also, the hybrid cost system may also be suitable for some basic cost management such as variance analysis to indicate services that are using a high proportion of overhead resources. Additional sources of variation in cost accounting have been traced to organizational factors that are discussed in the next section. Future research is needed to look at the factors that contribute to the wide variation in cost accounting practices of governments.

Cost Accounting Theories

Unlike the lack of description in the literature on cost accounting in government, there is a large degree of theoretical development around cost accounting in business and for-profit organizations. There is much less theoretical development specifically to governmental cost accounting. It remains to be tested how much of it applies to government and public organizations, but the net is cast wide in this literature review to develop a broad potential theoretical base on which a future research on government cost accounting could draw. The review of the theories first focuses on the most commonly used theories and then focuses on theories that have been applied specifically to government and semipublic organizations.

Common Social Science Theories and Their Relationship to Cost Accounting

Contingency Theory

Contingency theory has been applied extensively as a descriptive theory in the managerial accounting literature. Dating back to early attempts to build a descriptive theory of cost and managerial accounting (Hayes, 1977; Tiessen & Waterhouse, 1983) and building off the work of contingency theory in organization and management science (Lawrence & Lorsh, 1967; Thompson, 1967), contingency theory underpins much of the literature that has looked at how cost and managerial accounting is used and practiced. In spite of the many contributions of contingency theory, challenges remain, and there remains little work on government or not-for-profit cost accounting outside of health care in the United States.

In a wonderful synthesis of the contingency literature on management control systems, which is a broader classification that includes cost and managerial accounting, Chenhall (2003) notes that there is a long history of contingency theory in the discipline. He breaks up the literature into works that have looked at how factors influence some aspect of cost accounting, such as its use or implementation, and studies that have looked at how cost accounting leads to some other outcome, such as information or performance. He notes that most of the literature has been focused on the factors that influence the systems and much less has looked at how the cost accounting leads to outcomes. When the literature has looked at the outcomes of managerial cost systems, it is mostly to look at whether necessary information is being provided. The assumption is that better information and better decisions will lead to better performance. However, measuring the performance effects of better information is difficult given that most private organizations are in fairly competitive marketplaces and should already be at an optimum for their organization and their market. This uncomfortable outcome in competitive, private organizations, though, provides an opportunity for research in public organizations.

The Chenhall synthesis breaks the literature into three main groups of generic variables that relate to the original, organizational contingency theory: environment, technology, structure-strategy. Only the first generic contingency theoretic grouping has had any sort of empirical testing in public organizations. Geiger and Ittner (1996) show that funding by user charges promotes cost accounting development in federal agencies and Mohr (2015) shows that a similar relationship is likely to exist in local governments as well. In private businesses, a competitive (Kaplan & Cooper, 1998) or "turbulent and hostile" environment is thought to increase cost accounting and formal controls. Certainly, the environment for local government has been hostile for local governments as tax revenues have been taken away, and local governments have had to rely more on user charges. Interestingly, Chenhall asserts that a more uncertain environment is likely to promote "more open and externally focused" systems. These conflicting expectations surrounding uncertain and turbulent/hostile environments may be one reason why there has not been a clear shift to more cost accounting in public organizations.

A generic technology set of variables from the organization and management literature defines the relevant dimensions of technology as complexity, uncertainty, and interdependence. In the literature on public organizations, there is almost no literature on the task complexity, uncertainty, or interdependence as it relates to cost or managerial accounting (a forthcoming article by Mohr does look at task uncertainty in government cost accounting systems but in the context of transactions cost theory). Chenhall asserts that more complex tasks will promote formal control systems such as cost accounting and task uncertainty and interdependence will promote more informal control systems such as participatory budgeting.

Finally, Chenhall groups structure and strategy as important contingency theoretic categories. The original contingency theory issues of centralization, hierarchy, and size remain relevant. High technology and decentralized organizational structures seem to promote the use of cost accounting and formal control. More hierarchical organizations also promote the use of cost accounting because they have more levels of indirect costs and because they decentralize decision making in the organization (Geiger, 2000; Mohr, 2015). Size is not often tested, but Chenhall suggests that larger organizations are also likely to have more cost accounting. Finally, the strategies of managers should influence the use of cost accounting with managers who are more conservative or cost leaders are more likely to use cost and managerial accounting (Chenhall, 2003).

One area where contingency theory has been used extensively in cost accounting research is to look at the implementation of ABC. Anderson and Young (1999) give a thorough synthesis of that specific literature to that date. Their synthesis reveals that competition and uncertainty promote the implementation of ABC in five out of six studies. When it comes to task or technological characteristics, they note that risk and uncertainty were reported as negatively affecting implementation in three out of five studies but variety, worker autonomy, resource adequacy, and the availability of software promoted ABC implementation in three out of four studies. They note that organizational factors such as centralization and formalization promote ABC implementation (two studies). Finally, they note that individual characteristics also greatly influence how people perceive the implementation and usefulness of ABC.

Both the literature on all Management Control Systems (MCS) and the literature on specific cost accounting systems like ABC has made extensive use of contingency theory mostly in the context of private organizations. This literature can provide an extensive base upon which to build expectations about the use of cost accounting in public organizations. Chenhall notes that there are complications with the study of management accounting systems from a descriptive theory building perspective. Most important, the objects under study such as activity-based costing or balanced scorecards change over time. The meaning and development of the tools change, so he cautions the exclusive use of surveys and suggests that more qualitative work be done.

Agency Theory

Public financial management and public choice economics are imbued with principal-agent theory, which at first blush, would appear to provide a solid basis for empirical research into cost accounting in public organizations. The basic concept that principals that are charged with protecting the public's resources are likely to press for more cost accounting to hold the agents accountable. This mirrors the positive accountancy (Watts & Zimmerman, 1990) models of cost accounting that says that cost accounting is likely to be developed and used up to the point where the cost of measurement exceeds the cost of errors from incorrect cost information (Kaplan & Atkinson, 1998). Thus, the most straightforward theoretical prediction of agency theory is that principals can use cost accounting as a control for agency problems of ascertaining the cost of providing services.

Agency theory also maintains that agents are likely to shirk and use information asymmetry to avoid mechanisms of control (Dixit, 1997; Wilson, 1991). The theory comports with older observations that employees do not like to be controlled (Crozier, 1964) and particularly do not like to be accountable to costs, especially ones that they cannot control (Simon, Guetzkow, Kozmetsky, & Tyndall, 1954).

While the first part of agency theory is assumed in much of the literature on cost accounting and cost control, an elaborated agency theory that includes the shirking and information gaming of agents has not been extensively tested in a cost accounting context and especially for public cost accounting. Studies of ABC implementation imply that agents resist cost accounting and cost accounting development, but whether this resistance is related to shirking or sabotage is indeterminate. Flury and Schedler (2006) show that politicians in Switzerland want a fuller cost relative to managers, which is suggestive of the principal–agent dynamic. While there has been some work in this area, agency theory offers a potential but limited theoretic base given that task characteristics, environmental conditions, and other aspects of government structure appear to relate more directly to the different types of cost and managerial accounting practices that are often observed.

Transaction Cost Economics

A related theory to both agency theory and contingency theory is the transaction cost economics (TCE) or markets and hierarchies perspective (Coase, 1937; Williamson, 1985). TCE offers an important contextualization of the typical principal-agent role; whereby, the principles may not be able to fully measure costs because of the asset specificity and uncertainty surrounding services. Unfortunately, some studies that have applied TCE to cost accounting have concluded that it is not a sufficient theory for describing important cost accounting functions (Van Helden & Huijben, 2014).

The core idea of TCE is lock-in effect (Levin & Tadelis, 2010), whereby a principal becomes reliant on an agent for some particular skill or technology that the agent possesses (asset specificity) and the agent is reliant on the principal because the skill or technology is only applicable to the setting that is controlled by the principal. Both are shown to be made better off by working together, and more advanced governance arrangements are needed in such a situation (Williamson, 1985). The key variables in a transaction cost analysis are asset specificity, opportunism or uncertainty, and frequency or significance. The theory is nearly a contingency theory of the problems inherent in a principal–agent situation when the asset specificity is high and either the principal or agent can act opportunistically to exploit their partner. The theory also maintains that the transactions are also frequent or significant; otherwise, the potential loss may not be great enough to warrant extensive governance arrangements. Likewise, the theory also assumes bounded rationality. The theory is, thus, simplified to situations with high asset specificity and uncertainty are likely to have high transaction costs. As was previously maintained with the agency theory, the opportunistic behavior of agents to avoid extensive cost accounting may lead to excessive transaction costs to the organization and may reduce the probability of extensive cost accounting of asset specific services. Mohr (2013) also maintains that management may search to minimize uncertainty, which may lead to more cost accounting for services with uncertain outputs and outcomes.

In spite of the promise that transaction cost theory holds in public organizations (Williamson, 1999), the lock-in effect and asset specificity in TCE is mixed up with the employment contract and employment asset specificity, which Coase warns is problematic for the theory (Tadelis & Williamson, 2012, p. 9). Only two studies have used transaction cost theory to study managerial accounting in public organizations, and they either conclude that TCE is not a sufficient theory (Van Helden & Huijben, 2014) or that transaction cost effects can have different effects at different parts of the hierarchy of public organizations (Mohr, forthcoming). This implies that in a world of transaction costs that public services may not all be costed equally and that there are important questions about fairness when it comes to public costs. Indeed, one observer of government cost accounting has maintained that fairness in government cost accounting is on par with the cost and benefits of the system as a primary consideration in how cost accounting is developed in public organizations (Geiger, 2000, 2001). It is also important to remember that cost accounting is strongly associated with other structural aspects of the hierarchy of the organization, which may be endogenous to transaction costs. Therefore, the study of cost accounting in public organizations has a difficult task of untangling the effect of cost accounting from other structural effects of the hierarchy and the cost accounting system.

Other Relevant Theoretical Concepts and Their Relationship to Cost Accounting

Two other theoretical concepts, evolutionary theory and political/critical theory, are of note in the literature on cost accounting in public organizations. While they have not been developed as extensively in the mainstream cost accounting literature, they have been applied in public settings, which marks them as important. It is believed that these theories capture important and distinctive attributes of public organizations

Geiger's theory of the evolutionary cost accounting is reflected in the concept of hybrid cost accounting. When public organizations want to make changes to their cost accounting, they may not throw out their old system completely. If it was previously useful for purposes such as grant reporting, the cost accounting system may be kept and added upon to achieve new purposes like setting correct rates. Public organizations may find it hard to make a complete switch to ABC for the entire organization because it is too costly or because ABC runs into resistance in the organization. Therefore, Geiger proposes (2001) that cost accounting evolves in public organization toward a form that is more advanced or more like ABC. The evolutionary theory may thus be the mechanism by which the types of cost accounting that are seen in practice in many public organizations exhibit some characteristics of traditional cost accounting and some characteristics of ABC. However, few cost accounting systems that are widely used contain all the elements of ABC that were discussed previously.

A second consideration stems from the evolutionary nature of cost accounting in public organizations. If the cost accounting is evolving but not evolving equivalently in all the parts of the organization, it may create unequal cost estimates for some departments or services. Geiger (2001) maintains that fairness is also an important consideration for cost accounting in public organization beyond the rational or technocratic considerations of cost and benefit. In public organizations, there are likely to be winners and losers with any system, so considerations of fairness of the system may need to be balanced with the technically best choice.

Another way of saying that fairness is an issue with cost accounting is to say that it can also become political. Collier (2006) claims that the implementation of ABC to cost police services was used to switch panic over crime in Great Britain into one of panic regarding the cost of the police service. It is further claimed that these cost changes were used as a rhetorical device to affect the redistribution of police services and that the costing system served as a political tool to make these changes.

Related to the political theory is the use of critical theory when evaluating cost accounting innovations such as ABC. Jones and Dugdale (2002) use actor network theory to suggest that the creators of ABC were largely promoting a productivist ideology and that many of the innovations of ABC were abstracted from important local contexts. They note that the current "black box" nature of most corporate ABC limits a complete understanding of how it is actually being used, and it may not be living up to the hype that originally accompanied the tool. Indeed, much of the academic literature on ABC in government was critical of the tool. For example, Mullins and Zorn (1999) suggest that ABC leaves out important costs and benefits in the analysis of whether to contract out services. Anthony (1999) suggests that cost accounting information will not be used by many governments because the budgets tend to be on a cash basis, and others reflect that the cost might not outweigh the benefit (Williams & Melhuish, 1999).

These critical assessments may have been warranted in the 1990s as academics may have wanted to spare practitioners from what they felt were somewhat unnecessary and perhaps costly managerial experiments. The downside of these assessments is that it had a chilling effect on government cost accounting research. As will be noted in the next chapter on the history of cost accounting, these assessments and other challenges to cost accounting in the 1980s and 1990s stalled research on cost and managerial accounting in government. The result has been that practitioners have continued to evolve and experiment with cost accounting in new contexts and for new purposes given the difficult financial reality of the last couple decades for governments worldwide.

Conclusion

Developments in cost accounting since the advent of ABC more than 20 years ago have provided some new developments in cost accounting in public organizations. The review and the variety of cost accounting may be an interesting avenue for research into the often semantically difficult area of cost accounting and cost management in government. By analyzing relevant attributes of the cost accounting system (i.e., cost center, cost driver quality, and the number of cost drivers) an empirical research agenda may be developed around extant cost accounting practice that avoids the common academic constructions of cost accounting such as traditional cost accounting or ABC. While this research has not developed a framework for the influences on cost accounting development or sought to show how different cost accounting may influence important managerial decisions like the make–buy outsourcing decision, it shows that a large amount of variation exists in cost accounting practices, which can lead to differences in the perception of costs.

The field of cost accounting is one that is old by most standards of government budgeting research, but it is becoming more relevant as organizations search for ways to continue to manage their costs and recover resources in the presence of uncertain budgetary environments. New developments since ABC should focus attention on models of cost accounting that are not either ABC or traditional cost accounting but hybrid systems that have features of both. Given the importance of managing costs and the variation that exists in extant cost accounting systems, an empirical research agenda on different cost accounting practices is encouraged.

Notes

1　According to Kennet and coauthors in 2005, the number of cities that responded that they used ABC was less than 17%, and they suggest that this is likely a high estimate.

2　This section on traditional cost accounting is a general description of the characteristics of cost accounting. Interested readers who would like an applied description or examples of single-step-down, double-step-down methods, and even some simultaneous applications are referred to the Nashville-Davidson, *Cost Accounting Manual for Metro Government*, retrieved from http://www.nashville.gov/finance/omb/cost_accounting.asp. For a standard textbook description see Steven Finkler, *Financial Management for Public, Health, and Not-for-Profit Organizations*.

3　Guidelines for grants to local government from the federal government are found in 2 CFR Part 225, formerly OMB A-87.

4　Hypothetical examples are presented here to demonstrate important differences between the two ideal types of cost accounting and the important differences with the city cost accounting plans. It is important to note that cost plans outside of the federal government may be copyrighted material. Examples demonstrate the essential features, but interested readers should consult cost plans that are referenced.

5　It can be argued that traditional cost accounting systems can be used to help develop a more accurate estimate of the average cost of services. For example, the cost developed by the traditional cost accounting system can be divided by the total output of the department to derive an average cost for goods and services. In contrast, ABC uses specific drivers and a hierarchy of costs to approximate the marginal cost of services for management purposes that need more accurate service costs than those averaged across service types. However, averages of service costs are not the same as the more accurate estimates of individual service costs.

6　In this figure, I have noted the negative allocation for purposes of clarity. The allocation to receiving departments cancels out a cost in an overhead department. Also, I have noted the total cost that has been distributed to each level of service. In a larger example, all of the allocations would be combined at the end, but in the case of this simple example it shows how costs accumulate as each overhead department allocates its costs to service departments.

7　Jones and Dugdale (2002) note that there were at least two major types of ABC in the writing of Kaplan and coauthors. More recently, Kaplan and Anderson (2007) have even provided a new type of ABC called Time-Driven Activity-Based Costing (TDABC). The discussion presented in this section is a general description of the major considerations and differentiations between the traditional cost accounting and ABC. Readers interested in a more in-depth discussion of ABC and TDABC are referenced to the Kaplan and Anderson book and more recent work by Porter and Kaplan (2011), which has many follow-on studies in healthcare cost accounting.

8　See, for example, MGT Consulting Group (2016) Nashville-Davidson, Tennessee Federal 2 CFR Part 200 Central Services Cost Allocation Plan retrieved from http://www.nashville.gov/Finance/Management-and-Budget/Cost-Accounting-.aspx and MGT Consulting Group (2016) City Of Houston, Texas FY 2015 Full Cost Allocation Plan retrieved from www.houstontx.gov/finance/cost.html.

References

Anderson, S. W., & Sedatole, K. L. (2012). Evidence on the cost hierarchy: The association between resource consumption and production activities. *Journal of Management Accounting Research*, *25*(1), 119–141.

Anderson, S. W., & Young, S. M. (1999). The impact of contextual and process factors on the evaluation of activity-based costing systems. *Accounting, Organizations and Society*, *24*(7), 525–559.

Anthony, R. N. (1999). The fatal defect in the federal accounting system. *Public Budgeting & Finance*, *20*(4), 1–10.

Brimson, J. A., Antos, J., & Collins, J. (1999). *Driving value using activity-based budgeting*. New York: John Wiley and Sons.

Brown, R. E., Myring, M. J., & Gard, C. G. (1999). Activity based costing in government: Possibilities and pitfalls. *Public Budgeting & Finance*, *19*(2), 3–21.

Chenhall, R. (2003). Management control systems design within its organizational context: Findings from contingency-based research and directions for the future. *Accounting, Organizations and Society*, *28*(2–3), 127–168.

Coase, R. H. (1937). The nature of the firm. *Economica*, *4*(16), 386–405.

Collier, P. M. (2006). Costing police services: The politicization of accounting. *Critical Perspectives on Accounting*, *17*(1), 57–86.

Cooper, R., & Kaplan, R. S. (1988). Measure costs right: Make the right decisions. *Harvard Business Review*, *66*(5), 96–103.

Cooper, R., & Kaplan, R. S. (1992). Activity-based systems: Measuring the costs of resource usage. *Accounting Horizons*, *6*(3), 1–13.

Crozier, M. (1964). *The bureaucratic phenomenon*. Chicago, IL: University of Chicago Press.

Dixit, A. (1997). Power of incentives in private versus public organizations. *The American Economic Review*, 87(2), 378–382.

Finkler, S. A., Purtell, R., Calabrese, T., & Smith, D. (2012). *Financial management for public, health, and not-for-profit organizations* (4 ed.). Englewood Cliffs, NJ: Prentice Hall.

Flanagan, R., & Britain, G. (2008). *The review of policing: Final report*. London: Home Office.

Flury, R., & Schedler, K. (2006). Political versus managerial use of cost and performance accounting. *Public Money and Management*, 26(4), 229–234.

Geiger, D. R. (1999). Practical issues in cost driver selection for managerial costing systems. *The Government Accountants Journal*, 48(3), 32–39.

Geiger, D. R. (2000). *Winning the cost war: Applying battlefield management doctrine to the management of government*. Bloomington, IN: iUniverse Star.

Geiger, D. R. (2001). Practical issues in avoiding the pitfalls in managerial costing implementation. *The Journal of Government Financial Management*, 50(1), 26–34.

Geiger, D. R. (2010). *Cost management and control in government, fighting the cost war through leadership driven management*. New York: Business Expert Press.

Geiger, D. R., & Ittner, C. D. (1996). The influence of funding source and legislative requirements on government cost accounting practices. *Accounting, Organizations and Society*, 21(6), 549–567.

Goertz, G. (2006). *Social science concepts: A user's guide*. Princeton, NJ: Princeton University Press.

Gosselin, M. (1997). The effect of strategy and organizational structure on the adoption and implementation of activity-based costing. *Accounting, Organizations and Society*, 22(2), 105–122.

Hayes, D. C. (1977). The contingency theory of managerial accounting. *Accounting Review*, 52(1), 22–39.

Horngren, C., Datar, S., & Rajan, M. (2011). *Cost accounting: A managerial emphasis* (14 ed.). Englewood Cliffs, NJ: Prentice-Hall.

Johnson, H. T., & Kaplan, R. S. (1987). *Relevance lost: The rise and fall of management accounting*. Boston, MA: Harvard Business Press.

Jones, C. T., & Dugdale, D. (2002). The ABC bandwagon and the juggernaut of modernity. *Accounting, Organizations and Society*, 27(1–2), 121–163.

Kaplan, R. S. (1988). One cost system isn't enough. *Harvard Business Review*, 66(1), 61–66.

Kaplan, R. S., & Anderson, S. R. (2007). *Time-driven activity-based costing: A simpler and more powerful path to higher profits*. Boston, MA: Harvard Business Press.

Kaplan, R. S., & Atkinson, A. A. (1998). *Advanced management accounting* (Vol. 3). Englewood Cliffs, NJ: Prentice Hall.

Kaplan, R. S., & Cooper, R. (1998). *Cost & effect: Using integrated cost systems to drive profitability and performance*. Boston, MA: Harvard Business Press.

Kehoe, J. (1995). *Activity-based management in government*. Washington, DC: Coopers & Lybrand.

Kennett, D. L., Durler, M. G., & Downs, A. (2007). Activity-based costing in large US cities: Costs and benefits. *Journal of Government Financial Management*, 56(1), 20.

Kraines, O. (1970). The president versus congress: The keep commission, 1905–1909: First comprehensive presidential inquiry into administration. *The Western Political Quarterly, 23*(1), 5–54.

Lawrence, P., & Lorsh, J. (1967). *Organization and environment.* Cambridge, MA: Harvard Business Press.

Levin, J., & Tadelis, S. (2010). Contracting for government services: Theory and evidence from US cities *The Journal of Industrial Economics, 58*(3), 507–541.

Lienert, I. (2008). *Activity-based costing: Is it applicable in governments?* Retrieved from http://blog-pfm.imf.org/pfmblog/2008/11/activity-based.html

Martin, R. (2005). *Managerial cost accounting practices: Leadership and internal controls are key to successful implementation (GAO-05-1013R).* Washington, DC: United States Government Accountability Office.

Martin, R. (2007). *Managerial cost accounting practices: implementation and use vary widely across 10 federal agencies (GAO-07-679).* Washington, DC: United States Government Accountability Office.

Maximus. (2009). *City of Houston, Texas FY 2010 full cost allocation plan.* Retrieved from www.houstontx.gov/finance/cost.html

Mohr, Z. T. (2013). *Cost accounting in U.S. cities: Transaction costs and governance factors affecting cost accounting development and use.* Dissertation: University of Kansas.

Mohr, Z. T. (2015). An analysis of the purposes of cost accounting in large US cities. *Public Budgeting and Finance, 35*(1), 95–115.

Mohr, Z. T. (2016). Performance measurement and cost accounting: Are they complementary or competing systems of control? *Public Administration Review, 76*(4), 616–625.

Mohr, Z. (Forthcoming). Cost accounting at the service level: A transaction cost analysis. *Public Administration Quarterly.*

Mullins, D. R., & Zorn, C. K. (1999). Is activity based costing up to the challenge when it comes to privatization of local government services? *Public Budgeting & Finance, 19*(2), 37–58.

Porter, M., & Kaplan, R. (2011). How to solve the cost crisis in health care. *Harvard Business Rev, 89*(9), 46–64.

Premchand, A. (2006). Public expenditure management: Selected themes and issues. In H. Frank (Ed.), *Public financial management* (pp. 21–44). Boca Raton, FL: CRC Press.

Rivenbark, W. C. (2000). The art of using performance and cost data. *Local Finance Bulleting, 31*(1), 1–5.

Rivenbark, W. C. (2005). A historical overview of cost accounting in local government. *State & Local Government Review, 37*(3), 217–227.

Rivenbark, W. C., & Carter, K. L. (2000). Benchmarking and cost accounting: The North Carolina approach. *Journal of Public Budgeting Accounting and Financial Management, 12,* 125–137.

Robinson, M. (2007). Performance budgeting models and mechanisms. In M. Robinson (Ed.), *Performance budgeting: Linking funding and results* (pp. 1–18). New York: Palgrave Macmillan.

Rubin, I. S. (1993). Who invented budgeting in the United States? *Public Administration Review, 53*(5), 438–444.

Simon, H. A., Guetzkow, H., Kozmetsky, G., & Tyndall, G. (1954). Centralization vs decentralization in organizing the controller's department. In R. Golembiewski &

J. Rabin (Eds.), *Public budgeting and finance* (4 ed., pp. 203–210). New York: Marcel Dekker.

Tadelis, S., & Williamson, O. (2012). Transaction cost economics. In R. Gibbons & J. Roberts (Eds.), *Handbook of organizational economics* (pp. 159–192). Princeton, NJ: Princeton University Press.

Thompson, J. D. (1967). *Organizations in action: Social science bases of administrative theory.* New York: McGraw-Hill.

Tiessen, P., & Waterhouse, J. H. (1983). Towards a descriptive theory of management accounting. *Accounting, Organizations and Society, 8*(2), 251–267.

Van Helden, G., & Huijben, M. (2014). Controlling overhead in public sector organizations. *International Journal of Public Sector Management, 27*(6), 475–485.

Watts, R. L., & Zimmerman, J. L. (1990). Positive accounting theory: A ten year perspective. *Accounting Review, 65*(1), 131–156.

Weiss, B. (1997). *Activity-based costing and management: Issues and practices in local government.* Chicago, IL: Government Finance Officers Association.

Williams, C., & Melhuish, W. (1999). Is ABCM destined for success or failure in the federal government? *Public Budgeting & Finance, 19*(2), 22–36.

Williamson, O. E. (1985). *The economic institutions of capitalism.* New York: Free Press.

Williamson, O. E. (1999). Public and private bureaucracies: A transaction cost economics perspective. *Journal of Law, Economics, and Organization, 15*(1), 306–342.

Wilson, J. (1991). *Bureaucracy: What government agencies do and why they do it.* New York: Basic Books.

2 Contextualizing Cost Accounting in Government From a Historical Perspective

Zachary T. Mohr and William C. Rivenbark

Recent work has shown that cost accounting has been an important part of government financial management since at least the turn of the 20th century (Rivenbark, 2005; Williams, 2004). The research has shown that at different periods, it has been important for budgeting, accounting, and performance measurement. In spite of its historical significance, it has never been a completely unifying financial management tool that some have projected it to be (Premchand, 2006). This chapter looks to contextualize cost accounting from the lens of history and to see what cost accounting tools or techniques developed during different periods. It also seeks to understand why cost accounting has struggled to live up to its potential to support various aspects of government financial management.

To achieve these research objectives, we start by asking two basic questions about cost accounting in government. First, what are the stages and major developments of cost accounting? Second, in spite of its early promise and use, why has cost accounting been historically "limited" in achieving its potential? We explore the history of cost accounting with three distinct stages in response to the first objective: the early years (1885–1940), the technical years (1941–1970), and the modern years (1971–present). We then present a conceptual model of the relationship between cost accounting and other financial management tools that suggests both the reasons for its use and why it has received less attention in the modern years.

The Early Years: 1885–1940[1]

Although modern methods of cost accounting were introduced in the United States during the 1800s, the use of cost accounting in such countries as England, Germany, and Italy is documented as early as the 14th century (Brown, 1905; Garner, 1954). Most scholars cite Henry Metcalf's *Cost of Manufactures* (1885) as the turning point of cost accounting in the United States (Previts & Merino, 1979, 1998). As a captain in the United States Army, Metcalf used governmental workshops to explore the value of cost accounting by reporting on fixed and variable costs (Garner, 1954). While Metcalf is known as the father of cost accounting in the United States, one of his contemporaries, Fredrick R. Clow, is often cited as the father of cost accounting in local government.

Three major contributions to the study and practice of local government finance are found in the work of Clow (1896). He expanded the work of the prominent Prussian institutional economist Adolf Wagner (Fox, 1977) and offered an expenditure classification system, which eventually became the basis for governmental accounting. The second major contribution is in the area of cost accounting. Clow (1896) recognized the distinction between ordinary or "current" expenditures for service provision and extraordinary expenditures of debt payments and capital outlay.[2] His interest in this area came from the desire to track efficiency trends over time and to make efficiency comparisons among multiple jurisdictions. His third contribution is from the recognition that an independent organization was needed to develop and support professional standards of local government finance. He recommended that the National Municipal League, which was founded in 1894, take the lead role in this area (Previts & Merino, 1979).

The National Municipal League published a declaration of new principles for municipal reform in 1899, responding to the progressive movement and to the growth rate in local government (Fox, 1977). Building on the work of Clow (1896), the National Municipal League promoted "functional" city government and advocated uniformity and comparability in municipal accounting and financial reporting (Fox, 1977). This occurred during the same time the Federal Bureau of Labor was responsible for collecting and publishing city statistics regarding cost-of-service provision and units of efficiency (Meyer, 1910).

The Federal Census Bureau was created in 1902 and given the responsibility for the collection and publication process of city statistics in jurisdictions of over 30,000 in population (Meyer, 1910). The Census Bureau advanced the work of the Bureau of Labor and the National Municipal League to become a primary agent of accounting reform in municipal government (Woodruff, 1908). It also organized a meeting of municipal finance officers to discuss the adoption of a uniform system of accounting in 1903, which ultimately resulted in the creation of the Municipal Finance Officers Association (MFOA) in 1906 (Rivenbark & Allison, 2003). The MFOA, which eventually became the Government Finance Officers Association (GFOA), sponsored special committees throughout its early history to establish GAAP until the GASB was created in 1984 and assumed this responsibility.[3]

Meyer (1910) suggested that the major problem faced by the Census Bureau at the turn of the 20th century was the collection and publication of city statistics. The Census Bureau responded in 1910 by deciding that unit cost accounting as recently developed in the private sector could be modified to suit the needs of government (Fox, 1977). W. F. Willoughby, the assistant director of the Census Bureau at that time, felt that true progress toward increasing the efficiency of municipal government could only be made by comparing financial inputs with physical outputs in order to calculate unit cost of service delivery (Fox, 1977). While the work of the Census Bureau promoted the development and use of cost accounting in local government (Walker, 1930), problems remained from the standpoint of comparability.

Stephen (1939) criticized the Census Bureau for using the term "governmental-cost payments" rather than "governmental costs." Stephens contended that unit costs among cities were not comparable because disbursements (cash payments), expenditures (incurrence of liabilities), and costs (value of goods and services consumed) were not being interpreted consistently across jurisdictions. He argued that the Census Bureau's choice of terms contributed to the problem. Stephen's (1939) work focused primarily on how cost accounting would improve the annual preparation and adoption process of local government budgeting. He maintained that cost accounting systems must be coordinated with general accounting systems for accuracy, providing detail on how cost accounting would be integrated with the budget function.[4]

The MFOA appointed a national committee on cost accounting in 1939 to conduct exploratory work in the field (Wilson, 1940). The committee's work made two important contributions to the study and practice of cost accounting in local government. It represented the only known systematic compilation of available information on the subject at that time in the United States, and it provided principles and techniques for further consideration.

The 1939 committee also explored the usefulness of cost data to local government (efficiency analysis, policy determination, establishment of service fees, budgeting, personnel management, and public reporting) and identified three options for implementing cost accounting in local government: independent of the general ledger and managed at the functional level; operated outside of the general ledger but reconciled on a periodic basis; or subsidiary of the general accounting system and balanced with control accounts. The committee favored the third option given the ongoing accuracy required for meaningful cost information (Wilson, 1940).

The committee concluded that cost accounting had been adopted only in isolated cases in local government. The few areas of local government that utilized cost accounting on an ad hoc basis included public works, schools, hospitals, and libraries (Wilson, 1940). The proponents of cost accounting between 1885 and 1940 advocated its utility in local government on the strength of calculating the unit costs-of-service provision. Wilson (1940) noted, however, that the cost of implementing cost accounting had to be determined and compared against the benefits of cost accounting similar to any other recommended management innovation.

The recent research on the evolution of performance measurement offers additional insight to the early years of cost accounting. Williams (2003, 2004) noted that the work of the New York Bureau of Municipal Research during the early 20th century was instrumental in developing performance capacity in local government, including the collection and dissemination of measures involving output, outcome, and efficiency. The bureau focused on classifying data into functions so that cost could be determined and compared, including how these costs were associated with results and administrative efficiency. The bureau's efforts apparently influenced the landmark work of Clarence E. Ridley and Hebert A. Simon (1937) on performance measurement in local government.

Many other prominent figures influenced the thinking on cost accounting and on the efficiency of service delivery in public organizations during this era. Haskins and Cleveland (1904) examined the efficiency of consolidation in municipal government and promoted the profession of accountancy in theory and practice. Cooke (1919) advocated for improved financial methods in municipal government—which included budget and cost systems that provided information on work efficiency and economy—and supported the principles of scientific management as outlined by Frederick W. Taylor as an approach to better municipal government.[5]

The Technical Years: 1941–1970[6]

The individuals writing about cost accounting in local government during the middle of the 20th century focused primarily on how to implement it. Building on the work of the national committee on cost accounting appointed by the MFOA (Wilson, 1940), advocates of cost accounting published their work primarily in professional journals and were adamant that cost accounting would only be successful if integrated with the general accounting system with subsidiary-controlled accounts (Kimpel, 1944; Lorig, 1950). The major reasons for this integration were that cost accounting systems required an even greater degree of accuracy than did general accounting systems (Lorig, 1950); controlled accounts for tracking costs had to be reconciled with expenditure accounts for reporting meaningful and reliable information; and cost data involved the recasting of financial data for calculations of unit costs (Pelham, 1950). Although the writers of this period agreed on the integration of general and cost accounts and on the need for cost accounting in local government, there were significant variations on how they approached the details.

Kimpel (1944) suggested that those outside the municipal financial offices were promoting the adoption of cost accounting to a greater degree than those inside the offices. Some 60 years later, this observation might also apply to the recent passage of Statement No. 34 by the GASB, where local finance officials were not generally supportive of the changes in the general-purpose external financial reporting model. Kimpel insisted that cost accounting should only be implemented if the cost results were actually going to be used by the operating officials. He also noted that certain conditions could be identified for implementing cost accounting outside the central finance office. In other words, Kimpel hedged on the notion that cost accounting systems would only be successful unless integrated with general accounting systems.

Roberts' (1948) contribution to cost accounting comes from his description of management steps that precede the actual accumulation of cost data. These steps involve trained personnel, organizational structure and work assignment, identification of work units, reporting system for results, and continuous program for methods improvement. This framework is similar to the various frameworks of performance measurement being promoted today. Even the continuous program for methods improvement is now being recognized as critical to performance statistics where performance data are audited or verified for the end goal of improving the integrity of performance measurement systems (Rivenbark & Pizzarella, 2002; Williams, 2003). Roberts (1948) also addressed the organizational capacity needed for implementing and managing an effective cost accounting system—an area of performance budgeting currently receiving attention (Kelly & Rivenbark, 2003).

A contribution made to cost accounting by Riehl (1948) comes from his view on charging out general overhead to functional areas of service delivery. He promoted the technique of calculating the total cost of administrative overhead and distributing it among organizational functions based on a general methodology rather than on the basis of more rigorous and costly methods currently advocated for activity-based costing (Brown, Myring, & Gard, 1999). He also suggested that cost accounting allowed public providers to compare their services directly against private providers on a periodic basis through the bidding process. This is one of the first hints of the current initiative known as managed competition.

Another area of financial management that received attention during this era was increasing the professionalism of budget preparation and execution. Buck (1948) identified seven areas that would enhance the control process of budget execution, which included periodic departmental reports. These reports, however, would provide more than budget-to-actual expenditure variances. They would include departmental accomplishments as demonstrated by units of measurement—such as tons of refuse collected and gallons of water pumped—and unit cost by dividing total cost by the units accomplished. Buck (1948) concluded that the variations in unit cost over time would provide the signal for executive action.

Alice John Vandermeulen published an article in *Public Administration Review* in 1950 that combined the theoretical application of measuring efficiency with the technical treatment of cost accounting found in professional journals. Expanding on the work of Ridley and Simon (1937), Vandermeulen (1950) argued that efficiency should be approached within the context of how it is going to be used. The basic measure of efficiency is cost per unit and is used for the purpose of direct comparison. Another approach to efficiency is measuring the quality of service, which is now commonly known as effectiveness or outcome measures (Ammons, 2001). The final approach to efficiency described by Vandermeulen (1950) is its relation to the service goal. Because efficiency is relative and citizens may want a higher level of service, it must be analyzed in the context of how service provision is structured.

The MFOA published a symposium in 1950 in an effort to heighten the awareness of cost accounting in local government. The articles provided information on the use of control accounts (Lorig, 1950), on how to recast expenditure data into cost data (Pelham, 1950), on how to calculate the full cost of public works (Rowe & Miller, 1950), on how to calculate the full cost of office operations (Cope, 1950), and on how to build the budget around unit costs of service delivery (Brighton, 1950). However, there were two inconsistencies within the symposium.

The first involved the budget process. Lorig (1950) promoted a methodology for controlled accounts that would not interfere with budgetary accounts. Brighton (1950), on the other hand, promoted a process where the unit cost of each work program multiplied by the estimated units for the following fiscal year would yield the budget. The second inconsistency involves the approach to cost accounting. Cope (1950) presented a managerial accounting approach for an overall analysis of service provision while the other authors approached cost accounting from the utility of measuring efficiency.

The application of cost accounting between a methodology for calculating unit costs of service delivery and an initiative for supporting the broader framework of managerial accounting continued during the technical years. Senecal (1952) maintained that cost accounting is "as necessary to public administration as it is to private business to insure [sic] efficiency in administration and economy in expenditures" (p. 77). He also suggested that performance standards are measurements of the quantity of work and not the quality of work, reflecting a common view of the period that efficiency was "the" driver of administration. Takasaki (1962), on the other hand, recommended that the proper way to approach efficiency in government is to differentiate between technical and valued efficiency. Technical efficiency is more suited for the production of goods. Valued efficiency deals with ambiguous services that are demanded by citizens. Using a managerial approach to cost accounting, Takasaki (1962) promoted a framework of quarterly reporting in local government based on socioeconomic analysis, budget analysis, and performance analysis.

The National Committee on Governmental Accounting (NCGA) also promoted the use of cost accounting during this era as evidenced in *Municipal Accounting and Auditing* of 1951. This publication represents the second edition of the Blue Book, which was originally published by the National Committee on Municipal Accounting and is now published by the GFOA (Gauthier, 2012). The NCGA included an accounting principle in the 1951 Blue Book that advocated for cost accounting systems. However, the principle was removed before the NCGA published the third edition of the Blue Book in 1968—*Governmental Accounting, Auditing, and Financial Reporting*.

Common themes during the technical years were that the need for cost accounting in local government was evident, the numerous uses of cost accounting would greatly improve the management functions of public administration, and the research and focus on cost accounting would intensify as more jurisdictions implemented systems to accurately account for the total cost of service delivery. Roberts (1948) suggested that in "the vast field of governmental activities we have reached the point when expenditures should be justified in specific terms of volume of service per dollar expended" (p. 15). The promoters of cost accounting during this era had clearly set the stage for the next steps of cost accounting: its widespread implementation and use in local government.

The Modern Years: 1971–Present

During the early years cost accounting techniques were important for establishing accounting and in the technical years it was applied to budgeting in public organizations. In the modern years, new budgeting systems would disconnect cost accounting from the mainstream of budgeting. Cost accounting maintained a connection with the accounting function, particularly for lower levels of government that received federal grants. The new connection for cost accounting would come with the relationship to performance measurement and management.

Budgeting

During the technical years, the idea of performance budgeting was a relatively simple proposition that suggested that the government needed only to figure out the optimal amount of goods and services to provide, and then multiply that amount by a unit cost to increase performance. This very simple system would rely heavily on cost accounting to determine the cost of the products and services, but figuring out an optimal output would prove much harder than the performance budgeting of the technical years suggested. This simplistic performance budgeting would give way to a more elaborate program planning and budgeting system (PPBS) in the late 1960s and 1970s. The implementation and shift of focus brought about by PPBS in the mid-1960s began to undo the cost accounting connection. By the 1970s the connection with budgeting would be further attenuated as other budget reforms like zero-based budgeting and management by objectives no longer considered indirect costs.

While cost accounting was not specifically central to the program and planning budget agenda, it is important to remember that cost accounting was not forgotten at this point. Indeed, the early reformers realized that indirect costs (Frank, 1973) and cost accounting were critically important for determining the cost of government programs. In the ideal program budgeting system, the budget agency knows the total direct and indirect costs of a program. From there, the chance to plan a socially optimal set of programs can take place. Unfortunately, Frank (1973) notes that the assignment of indirect costs never took place in most PPBS systems.

Robert Anthony, the well-known management accounting scholar, was the comptroller in the Defense Department at this time and notes that the assignment of depreciation expense and indirect costs had been a major objective of military financial management since the time of the first Hoover Commission in 1949. However, the Appropriations Committee would not consider a budget that was not on a cash basis and in conformance with how the government obligates money (Anthony, 1999). Whether it was because the legislative branch refused to budget on a total cost basis or the program budgeting exercise was rushed into other federal agencies, there has never been a coherent system for aggregating programmatic costs and assigning the indirect costs that are necessary to provide the services.

Later budgetary reforms, like zero-based budgeting, would completely neglect that indirect costs were important. The zero-base budgeting idea that budgets can be restarted from zero does not need to consider whether the budget is connected to other resources because those resources are zeroed out and then rejustified by needs. Of course, other budgetary reforms of the period had additional problems besides not providing better information on the true cost of services, but most important, for the use of cost accounting in government, the use of cost accounting and indirect cost allocation was not used much in practice after the early years of the modern era.

Cost Accounting Standards and Circulars

By the mid-1970s, cost accounting was no longer aligned strongly with budgeting for most governments in the United States, but it became more relevant for financial reporting. Especially as the federal government did away with the block grant system, targeted grants to state and local governments require cost accounting to account for the indirect cost when providing services from federal grants at the state and local levels. Especially in a large and varied country like the United States, cost accounting for indirect and overhead costs in local government was difficult to standardize and remains complicated (see Chapter 5 of this book for relevant aspects of government cost accounting for grants).

In 1968 the NCGA backed off from a municipal cost accounting standard. While it had attempted to advocate for cost accounting in earlier editions of the "Blue Book," the third edition abandoned attempts to prescribe a government cost accounting standard. Today, the GASB does not have a standard on indirect costs allocated in financial statements. It does, however, give guidance on the use of internal service funds and it allows for the presentation of indirect costs in the government-wide financial statements. Additionally, with the passage of GASB Statement 34, the assignment of depreciation expense in the government-wide statements provides a somewhat fuller expense for the broad categories of activities that are justified in the statement of activities, but it does not account for other resources that are used in other departments to provide a good or service. For a brief time, it was thought that Statement 34 would reignite interest in cost accounting for government services, but this has not been the case since Statement 34 was implemented in the early 2000s.

Only the federal government has a current cost accounting standard. FASAB Standard 4, adopted in 1995, adopts managerial cost accounting for the federal government. However, even a cursory read of this standard reveals that it is much more of an intention or aspiration than an objective standard. Since the creation of this standard, the Government Accountability Office has consistently found that improvements are needed to agencies' cost accounting systems (Martin, 2005, 2007).

While local governments during this time were not able to systematize their cost accounting through typical accounting standards and the federal government would only pass a weak standard much later, the system that the federal government promoted to account for the indirect costs of grant overhead would promote more standardized cost accounting throughout the United States for state and local governments.

The Bureau of the Budget (BoB, now the Office of Management and Budget, or OMB) issued the first A-87 circular in 1968. In it they specify the cost accounting standards necessary for the federal government to reimburse state and local governments. Prior to A-87, the different federal agencies had issued their own cost accounting guidelines, which started in 1947 with the Office of Naval Research (ONR) issuing guidance on determining indirect cost rates for educational institutions. Since educational institutions and the ONR were quite unique, this led to the A-21 circular in 1958, which was similar in intent to the A-87.[7]

This bifurcation of cost accounting standards seems to be an important aspect of cost accounting, as the determination of the "allowable costs" is split between different agencies of the federal government. In the original A-87 cost standards, the provision for determining allowable costs at the "state level" was delegated to the Department of Health, Education, and Welfare. Other granting federal agencies were compelled to follow the cost allocation plans that were approved by the department. At the local level (cities and counties), it was not as straightforward because communities were engaged in very different federal activities with some getting large grants and contracts for road construction, others doing large-scale urban renewal efforts, and others providing significant human services.[8] These differing tasks have different types of indirect costs that are allowed by cost standards. Therefore, the original cost accounting provided only that the cost accounting plans of local government by "a single Federal agency, the one with predominant interest . . . for the negotiation and approval of the cost allocation plan and for the audit of costs" (Hughes, 1968, p. 7). Eventually, these cost accounting approval agencies would become the *cognizant* agency that approved the cost accounting plans. By 1980 OMB had issued an extensive list in the Federal Register (Vol. 45 No. 41) that extensively listed all of the major cities' cognizant agencies.

While the separation and multiplication of cost accounting cognizant agencies by 1980 did not help standardize cost accounting, the issuance of standards did help to standardize the language and practices (see also Chapter 5 of this book). Another major development was the use of for-profit consulting services that used standardized cost accounting programs to create more standardized cost accounting. By the 1980s, cost accounting and cost accounting plans were much more standardized among the many diverse types of organizations and communities that were responsible for following federal cost accounting standards. Additionally, these plans and their indirect cost rates were much more aligned with financial reporting and auditing than they were with budgeting for the programs.

It should be noted that the government also has cost accounting standards for companies (48 CFR 99). This 218-page regulation provides extensive cost accounting requirements for projects over $700,000, where the company has a total contract value with the federal government over $7.5 million. The Cost Accounting Standards Board, which oversees private sector contract cost accounting, was established in 1970, eliminated in 1981, and reestablished in 1988 (Bales, 2015).

Performance Management

While the modern years have been largely a time of standardization for cost accounting practice, the financial stress and competition for resources in the 1980s would provide challenges to cost accounting generally, and government cost accounting experienced its own specific problems associated with the political nature of government service costs. The primary solution to the general challenge was Activity-Based Costing (ABC). As was argued in Chapter 1 of this book, ABC is more advanced and allows allocation to more specific cost objects, but it was criticized for its use in government. Other practical and theoretical challenges in the 1980s would also weaken the legitimacy of cost accounting in government. In spite of the many challenges during this period, cost accounting connected with performance measurement and management.

The late 1970s and early 1980s were a period of global competition for businesses in the United States. It is generally discussed that it was this period of intense competition that forced businesses to improve their cost accounting procedures in the late 1980s and 1990s (Johnson & Kaplan, 1987; Kaplan & Cooper, 1998). ABC became synonymous with cost accounting in the 1990s. One survey of local governments during the mid-1990s revealed that over half (50.8%) of local governments had implemented ABC (Shih-Jen & Kidwell, 2000).

In spite of the widespread interest, ABC was criticized heavily for its uses in government. As was discussed in Chapter 1 of this book, scholars of government financial management noted that it was inappropriate for government budgeting and contracting, and it was often more expensive than it was worth. While these challenges were well founded, they also ignored that ABC was being used by many different types of governments to help them improve their operations and reduce costs (Brimson & Antos, 1994; Geiger, 2000; Kaplan & Anderson, 2007; Weiss, 1997). Even though the ABC system often helped show where efficiencies could be made, the governments often abandoned the system when the easiest efficiencies were made, when external financial pressures were reduced, or because of changes in leadership. One of the most notable examples of ABC success in the 1990s was the City of Indianapolis that used ABC to find services that were much more expensive than could be purchased from the market. ABC clearly showed where efficiencies could be made and by a mixture of process improvement and managed competition the city was able to make several operations more efficient (Weiss, 1997). By the mid-2000s, Indianapolis was not extensively using ABC, most notably because Stephen Goldsmith was no longer the mayor. The city also was experiencing less financial stress and the easiest improvements had been made. Unless cost accounting is tied very specifically to relevant performance measurements, the simple fact is that governments do not have the intense financial competition of business to drive further cost accounting improvements (Kennett, Durler, & Downs, 2007). This makes it possible for a government to ignore costs when financial times are less challenging. In 2005, a survey of United States cities showed that fewer than 17% were using or considering using ABC, and this was likely a high estimate due to the sampling procedures and response characteristics of the cities (Kennett et al., 2007). If the Ho and Kidwell survey in 1995 was representative, this means that almost two thirds of cities that were using ABC in the mid-1990s had abandoned the tool in less than a decade.

The political nature of cost accounting cannot be underestimated and may, in fact, be another reason that governments have shied away from extensive cost accounting. The $400 hammer in the 1980s was a major political scandal for the Department of Defense. The hammer was, in fact, a cost object in a much-larger Research and Development (R&D) purchase, but because extensive engineering overhead was passed down to all direct expenditures, it made it look like the hammer was much more expensive than it was. It is difficult to tell how much political scandals have hindered cost accounting in government, but they have been a challenge for governments in a way that businesses simply do not have to consider. When ABC was used to manage local police forces in Great Britain, the use of the tool was thought to be politically motivated, and it was charged that it was biased even against public purposes broadly (Collier, 2006; Jones & Dugdale, 2002).

These practical challenges to cost accounting during this period have been marked mostly by a decline in interest among academics on the subject. In a recent survey, over two thirds of large cities in the United States were using cost accounting when it was broadly defined (Mohr, 2015), and many local government practitioners in the United State are familiar with cost accounting (Mohr, 2013). This suggests that cost accounting remains an important topic for practitioners in spite of a large gap in the literature on cost accounting in the United States. In fact, between the symposium in *Public Budgeting and Finance* that condemned the use of ABC in government and the recent articles by Mohr (2015, 2016), there was only one article on the specific subject that appeared in a government or public administration journal in the United States (Rivenbark, 2005). In academic managerial accounting journals, such as *Management Accounting Research* and *Journal of Management Accounting Research*, there were no articles published on government-specific cost accounting techniques or issues during the first decade of the century. One general conclusion from these observations is that academic interest in cost accounting has been extremely low recently, but practitioners continue to be interested in the topic.

The one area where continued interest in cost accounting has remained is in the area of performance management. Performance in government is a topic that has received widespread academic and practitioner attention over the last two decades. Projects such as Reinventing Government in the federal government and numerous local initiatives such as CitiStat, performance-based budgeting, and many others have greatly contributed to a widespread interest in government performance. Cost accounting is especially important to performance because it puts outcomes into comparative perspective and allows for better measures of efficiency (Mohr, 2016). Key to the connection between cost accounting and performance is the development of the Balanced Scorecard and standardized benchmarking regimes.

While Robert Kaplan is well known for ABC, he is equally known for the balanced scorecard (BSC), and the BSC has been extremely successful in government. The reason for this success is that the BSC measures four perspectives that are argued to each be essential for organizational success: business process perspective, the customer perspective, the learning and growth perspective, and the financial perspective (Kaplan & Norton, 1992). The BSC has been embraced vigorously by governments because they easily accept the need to reflect many different priorities in their performance evaluation. This has led governments throughout the world to adopt the BSC (Niven, 2008).

However, for governments the ABC and cost accounting approach may be even more fundamental for putting outcomes into perspective and creating better measures of efficiency. The problem for governments is that they do not have a profit for many of their activities, and this leads to a decision-making process that is more comparative. So, the budget for a community activity like parks or police is compared to other relevant communities. The only problem with comparing the performance of departments or services of cities with similar departments in other communities is that the budgeted amounts do not reflect the actual amount of resources that may be available to provide the service. For example, the fire departments in Community A might have expensive Geographic Information System (GIS) equipment and personnel included in their budget. In Community B, that GIS equipment and personnel might be in an individual department, and in Community C the GIS function may be housed in a separate department like public works. This makes evaluating the performance of the fire department in the three communities very difficult unless they have good cost accounting procedures. In essence, the resources that are available to produce services need to be equalized to make an apples-to-apples comparison of departmental or service performance in government. Unfortunately, some of the main benchmarking programs like the International City/County Management Association (ICMA) benchmarking program do not account for the incomparability of government departmental or service budgets (Coe, 1999).

Where this comparability of resources has been taken seriously is in the North Carolina Benchmarking Project, providing for uniform cost accounting for specific services that are of interest to communities in North Carolina. When the communities have uniform cost accounting procedures, they can make a direct comparison of their service performance to other communities' service performance because they can be assured that communities are not funding the service indirectly. This benchmarking process has been studied extensively and has shown to be highly beneficial to organizational learning and improvement (Ammons, 1995; Ammons & Rivenbark, 2008). This organizational improvement may most closely be aligned with the management of the organization's resources and budget implementation.

This new connection between government performance and cost accounting has been the main vehicle for academic interest in the topic of government cost accounting in the United States for the last two decades. While there were many potentially interesting things to study about ABC and cost accounting in government, the academic criticisms and political scandals during this era muted the interest for academic studies of actual cost accounting practices. The use of cost accounting and interest in it remain high from practitioners and especially by practitioners that are interested in putting organizational performance into comparative perspective.

Conceptualizing Cost Accounting's Relationships Over Time

In the previous sections, we suggest that government cost accounting has gone through three distinct periods of development. In contrast to other writers and commentators on cost accounting, we find that cost accounting in government has been limited over time and most recently because of a lack of alignment with the broader planning and reporting roles of budgeting and accounting. It has further been limited in government by political scandals and misperceptions. In spite of these historical limitations, cost accounting and related cost accounting techniques importantly shaped government budgeting and accounting, and continues to be highly relevant to providing government cost data for performance.

The historical record shows that cost accounting has been at its best when it has been most clearly aligned with the broader practices of budgeting and accounting (Figure 2.1). It has been the least relevant when it is not aligned with at least one of these practices. We suggest that, over time, cost accounting has been more associated with one or the other at any given time as if on a pendulum. We also suggest that the practice of performance measurement has solidified as an important practice that also is related to cost accounting over the last 100-plus years. The overlap of the subjects suggests the areas where cost accounting, financial accounting, budgeting, and performance have mutual areas of interest and can support one another. Figure 2.1 suggests that cost accounting and its related techniques are a critical if often overlooked aspect of government financial management, but it is important to note that these relationships have not been static over time.

In the early years, budgeting and accounting were still very much interrelated. Cost accounting techniques like activity analysis helped to establish the relevant categories of financial accounting and reporting. In the early years, cost accounting was very much aligned with accounting and unit costs were important. Cost accounting may have important relationships and provided capacity to governments in establishing early ideas about performance. Cost accounting and its techniques helped define and establish these areas of financial management practice for governments in the United States.

In the technical years, cost accounting became much more aligned with budgeting. Early interest in performance budgeting suggested using unit costs and optimal levels of output to budget efficiently. While these concepts of performance budgeting are generally considered much too simplistic for contemporary budgeting, cost accounting was critical for further establishing its relationship with budgeting and performance.

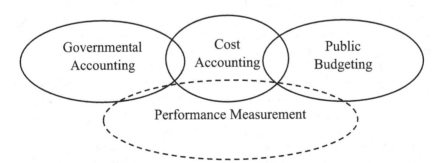

Figure 2.1 Connecting Cost Accounting With Budgeting, Accounting, and Performance Measurement

The modern years have been ones of both standardization and resistance to cost accounting. While cost accounting maintained a limited connection with accounting for federal grants, it became much less associated with budgeting. The overlap in the figure between budgeting and cost accounting became nearly nonexistent in practice besides for some minor uses for things like utility rate overhead recovery analyses (see Chapter 4 of this book). The area where cost accounting currently overlaps another area extensively is in the area of performance measurement and management (see Chapters 3 and 6 of this book for further discussion). In our diagram, performance measurement is symbolized by a dotted line to signify that performance was not a concrete idea for all three periods. We argue that it has really been in the modern years that performance measurement and management has become a solid and concrete practice. We believe that cost accounting currently overlaps and importantly contributes to performance measurement and management.

Overall, we conceptualize cost accounting as a pendulum swinging between budgeting and accounting with performance measurement and management additionally overlapping budgeting and accounting. Cost accounting has been at its most relevant when it has encompassed large areas of these three areas of practice. For cost accounting to become more relevant, the connections with accounting, budgeting, and performance should be strengthened.

Conclusion

In the introduction, we posed two basic questions about cost accounting: What are the major historical stages of cost accounting, and why has it been limited in its widespread adoption and use? To answer this in the context of governments in the United States, we split the periods into three major time frames. The first period showed that early cost accounting techniques were important tools for splitting the budget and resource planning functions from the financial reporting functions. Cost accounting was most widely used and discussed in the early 1950s when it was used extensively with early performance budgeting and maintained relevance for the accounting practices of state and local government. In the modern era, the use of cost accounting was disconnected from budgeting and had a limited connection with accounting, but it seems to have maintained a solid connection with performance measurement and management. Both political scandals and uncertainty about the type of cost accounting that is appropriate to use have recently limited widespread interest in the topic. Even though academics have been reluctant to study government cost accounting practices in recent years, interest in the subject among practitioners has remained high.

In conclusion, we would like to note that we continue to see relevance for the topic of government cost accounting. Most logically, cost accounting can strengthen its relationship to performance by organizations using efficiency and benchmarking techniques that can broadly benefit from good cost accounting. Government accounting can also broadly benefit from a more thorough discussion and guidance on this topic. Currently, indirect costs can be shown in the government-wide statements of state and local governments, but it is not known how many governments even do this. Finally, cost accounting and related techniques are important for budgeting to give citizens and elected officials a better idea of the cost of providing service. The departmental budget is usually a poor indicator of the true cost of service and is biased toward underestimation. It is uncertain how citizen engagement in the budgetary process would work without better estimates of cost than the usual departmental line-item budget. Additional connections to budgeting, accounting, and performance will ultimately enhance the credibility of cost accounting, but the inescapable need to account for the services, activities, and indirect costs of providing services are not likely to make cost accounting in government obsolete any time soon.

Notes

1 This section of the chapter is a reprint from the following article with the permission of SAGE Publications: William C. Rivenbark. (2005). A historical overview of cost accounting in local government. *State and Local Government Review*, 37(3), 217–227.

2 The distinction made by Clow (1896) between ordinary expenditures for service provision and extraordinary expenditures of debt payments and capital outlay is still a major area of focus for governmental and cost accounting. For example, capital outlay is captured as a direct expenditure in the governmental funds and accounted for with depreciation at the government-wide level as required by Statement No. 34. Adjustments to capital outlay are required at both reporting levels in order to calculate the cost of service provision, responding to the direct expenditure of capital assets at the fund level and to the aggregation of depreciation at the government-wide level.

3 The National Committee on Municipal Accounting was created in 1934 to establish and promulgate GAAP, which was replaced by the National Committee on Governmental Accounting in 1948. This committee ultimately was expanded and renamed the National Council on Governmental Accounting in 1973, which was replaced by the Governmental Accounting Standards Board in 1984. Because the Government Finance Officers Association is a professional organization, it has never directly established and promulgated GAAP.

4 Stephen (1939) also felt that the study of public finance was focused primarily on public revenues and that public expenditures received minimal consideration. "From this it may be readily assumed that within the science of public finance, the theory and practice of taxation is of greater importance than the theory and practice of public expenditures" (Stephen, 1939, p.7). The author felt that the narrow focus of public finance limited the development of public budgeting and cost accounting.

5 Cooke's work went beyond municipal government to include the roles of organization, management, and planning in private firms, which included the advancement of labor-management relations (Cooke & Murray, 1940).

6 This section of the chapter is a reprint from the following article with the permission of SAGE Publications: William C. Rivenbark. (2005). A historical overview

of cost accounting in local government. *State and Local Government Review,* 37(3), 217–227.

7 Danhof in *Government contracting and technological change* (Washington, DC: The Brookings Institution, 1965) notes that ONR stemmed from the Office of Scientific Research and Development (OSRD) that was created just prior to World War II. This board was responsible to the President and greatly expanded the use of private and public educational institutions to produce many of the successful research and development projects for the war. The OSRD was able to use expanded contracting powers from the War Powers Act of 1941 to provide some of the first federal government sponsored research on cost plus contracts. These cost plus fixed fee contracts are the contract mechanism that necessitates the cost accounting that is required for government contracts where overhead is reimbursed. Prior federal government discussion about cost accounting can be traced to the turn of the 20th century and the Keep Commission, where cost accounting ideas were discussed as an alternative way of funding the federal government relative to cash appropriations process, but this idea was ultimately abandoned for a simpler budget process (Oscar Kraines. [1970]. *The president versus congress: The keep commission, 1905–1909: First comprehensive presidential inquiry into administration*). Prior to the formalized use by ONR and OSDR after World War II, there is no evidence that cost accounting was used systematically in the federal government.

8 This also applies to specific departments of the state such as state departments of transportation that were "grantee department level" and were intended to follow the guidance of their primary granting agency such as the Department of Transportation (Ammons, 2001).

References

Ammons, D. N. (1995). Overcoming the inadequacies of performance measurement in local government: The case of libraries and leisure services. *Public Administration Review, 55*(1), 37–47.

Ammons, D. N. (2001). *Municipal benchmarks: Assessing local performance and establishing community standards.* London: Sage.

Ammons, D. N., & Rivenbark, W. C. (2008). Factors influencing the use of performance data to improve municipal services: Evidence from the North Carolina benchmarking project. *Public Administration Review, 68*(2), 304–318.

Anthony, R. N. (1999). The fatal defect in the federal accounting system. *Public Budgeting & Finance, 20*(4), 1–10.

Bales, A. F. (2015). *DCAA contract audit manual (DCAA Manual 7640.1).* Washington, DC: Defense Contract Audit Agency.

Brighton, G. R. (1950). Application of cost accounting to budgeting. *Municipal Finance Journal, 22*(3), 123–128.

Brimson, J. A., & Antos, J. (1994). *Activity-based management: For service industries, government entities, and nonprofit organizations.* New York: John Wiley and Sons.

Brown, R. (1905). *A history of accounting and accountants.* London: Ballantyne, Hanson & Company.

Brown, R. E., Myring, M. J., & Gard, C. G. (1999). Activity based costing in government: Possibilities and pitfalls. *Public Budgeting & Finance, 19*(2), 3–21.

Buck, A. E. (1948). Techniques of budget execution. *Municipal Finance, 21*(1), 8–11.

Clow, F. R. (1896). Suggestions for the study of municipal finance. *The Quarterly Journal of Economics, 10*(4), 455–466.

Coe, C. (1999). Local government benchmarking: Lessons from two major multi-government efforts. *Public Administration Review, 59*(2), 110–123.

Collier, P. M. (2006). Costing police services: The politicization of accounting. *Critical Perspectives on Accounting, 17*(1), 57–86.

Cooke, M. L. (1919). *Our cities awake*. Garden City, NY: Doubleday, Page & Company.

Cooke, M. L., & Murray, P. 1940. *Organized labor and production*. New York: Harper & Brothers.

Cope, O. K. (1950). Cost controls for office operations. *Municipal Finance, 22*(3), 117–122.

Fox, K. (1977). *Better city government*. Philadelphia, PA: Temple University.

Frank, J. E. (1973). A framework for analysis of PPB success and causality. *Administrative Science Quarterly, 18*(4), 527–543.

Garner, S. P. (1954). *Evolution of cost accounting to 1925*. Tuscaloosa, AL: University of Alabama Press.

Gauthier, S. J. (2012). *Governmental accounting, auditing, and financial reporting*. Chicago, IL: Government Finance Officers Association.

Geiger, D. R. (2000). *Winning the cost war: Applying battlefield management doctrine to the management of government*. Bloomington, IN: iUniverse Star.

Haskins, C. W., & Cleveland, F. A. (1904). *Business education and accountancy*. New York, NY: Harper & Brothers.

Hughes, P. S. (1968). *Principles for determining costs applicable to grants and contracts with state and local government (Circular No. A-87)*. Washington, DC: Bureau of the Budget.

Johnson, H. T., & Kaplan, R. S. (1987). *Relevance lost: The rise and fall of management accounting*. Boston, MA: Harvard Business Press.

Jones, C. T., & Dugdale, D. (2002). The ABC bandwagon and the juggernaut of modernity. *Accounting, Organizations and Society, 27*(1–2), 121–163.

Kaplan, R. S., & Anderson, S. R. (2007). *Time-driven activity-based costing: A simpler and more powerful path to higher profits*. Boston, MA: Harvard Business Press.

Kaplan, R. S., & Cooper, R. (1998). *Cost & effect: Using integrated cost systems to drive profitability and performance*. Boston, MA: Harvard Business Press.

Kaplan, R. S., & Norton, D. P. (1992). The balanced scorecard—measures that drive performance. *Harvard Business Review, 70*(1), 71–79.

Kelly, J. M., & Rivenbark, W. C. (2003). *Performance budgeting for state and local government*. Armonk, NY: ME Sharpe.

Kennett, D. L., Durler, M. G., & Downs, A. (2007). Activity-based costing in large US cities: Costs and benefits. *Journal of Government Financial Management, 56*(1), 20.

Kimpel, H. M. (1944). Cost accounting for municipalities. *Municipal Finance, 16*(4), 30–32.

Lorig, A. N. (1950). Integrating cost accounting with general accounting records. *Municipal Finance, 22*(3), 98–103.

Martin, R. (2005). *Managerial cost accounting practices: Leadership and internal controls are key to successful implementation (GAO-05–1013R)*. Washington, DC: United States Government Accountability Office.

Martin, R. (2007). *Managerial cost accounting practices: Implementation and use vary widely across 10 federal agencies (GAO-07–679)*. Washington, DC: United States Government Accountability Office.

Metcalf, H. (1885). *Cost of manufactures*. New York: John Wiley and Sons.

Meyer, E. C. (1910). The national census bureau and our cities. *Proceedings of the American Political Science Association*, Vol. 7, Seventh Annual Meeting, 126–137.

Mohr, Z. T. (2013). *Cost accounting in US cities: Transaction costs and governance factors affecting cost accounting development and use*. Dissertation: University of Kansas.

Mohr, Z. T. (2015). An analysis of the purposes of cost accounting in large US cities. *Public Budgeting and Finance*, 35(1), 95–115.

Mohr, Z. T. (2016). Performance measurement and cost accounting: Are they complementary or competing systems of control? *Public Administration Review*, 76(4), 616–625.

National Committee on Government Accounting. (1951). *Municipal accounting and auditing*. Chicago, IL: Municipal Finance Officers Association.

National Committee on Government Accounting. (1968). *Governmental accounting, auditing, and financial reporting*. Chicago, IL: Municipal Finance Officers Association.

Niven, P. (2008). *Balanced scorecard step-by-step for government and nonprofit agencies*. New York: John Wiley and Sons.

Pelham, A. M. (1950). Institutional cost accounting. *Municipal Finance*, 22(3), 106–112.

Premchand, A. (2006). Public expenditure management: Selected themes and issues. In H. Frank (Ed.), *Public financial management* (pp. 21–44). Boca Raton, FL: CRC Press.

Previts, G. J., & Merino, B. D. (1979). *A history of accounting in America*. New York: John Wiley and Sons.

Previts, G. J., & Merino, B. D. (1998). *A history of accountancy in the United States*. Columbus, OH: Ohio State University Press.

Ridley, C. E., & Simon, H. A. (1937). Technique of appraising standards. *Public Management*, 19(2), 46–49.

Riehl, E. P. (1948). Potential cost accounting applications. *Municipal Finance*, 21(1), 53–56.

Rivenbark, W. C. (2005). A historical overview of cost accounting in local government. *State & Local Government Review*, 37(3), 217–227.

Rivenbark, W. C., & Allison, G. S. (2003). The GFOA and professionalism in local government. *The Journal of Public Budgeting, Accounting & Financial Management*, 15(2), 228–238.

Rivenbark, W. C., & Pizzarella, C. M. (2002). Auditing performance data in local government. *Public Performance & Management Review*, 25(4), 413–420.

Roberts, S. M. (1948). Management responsibility for cost accounting. *Municipal Finance*, 20(3), 14–18.

Rowe, W. E., & Miller, W. C. (1950). Cost accounting for public works. *Municipal Finance*, 22(3), 113–116.

Senecal, C. A. (1952). Imperative need for cost accounting in government. *Municipal Finance*, 25(2), 76–78.

Shih-Jen, K. H., & Kidwell, L. A. (2000). A survey of management techniques implemented by municipal administrators. *The Journal of Government Financial Management*, 49(1), 46.

Stephen, A. H. F. (1939). *Possibilities of the use of cost accounting in public budget making.* Dissertation: University of Pennsylvania.

Takasaki, R. S. (1962). Measuring efficiency in government. *Municipal Finance, 34*(4), 145–149.

Vandermeulen, A. J. (1950). Guideposts for measuring the efficiency of governmental expenditures. *Public Administration Review, 10*(1), 7–12.

Walker, M. L. (1930). *Municipal expenditures.* Baltimore, MD: Johns Hopkins University Press.

Weiss, B. (1997). *Activity-based costing and management: Issues and practices in local government.* Chicago, IL: Government Finance Officers Association.

Williams, D. (2003). Measuring government in the early twentieth century. *Public Administration Review, 63*(6), 643–659.

Williams, D. (2004). Evolution of performance measurement until 1930. *Administration & Society, 36*(2), 131.

Wilson, F. B. (1940). Municipal cost accounting. *Municipal Finance, 12*(4), 26–41.

Woodruff, C. R. (1908). *Pittsburgh conference for good city government.* Washington, DC: National League of Cities.

3 The Intrinsic Value of Cost Accounting for Benchmarking Service Efficiency

William C. Rivenbark

The push for performance measurement in local government can be traced back to the early 1900s, when the New York Bureau of Municipal Research recognized the need for data-driven decision making and began promoting the documentation of outputs and outcomes of service delivery (Williams, 2003). The modern push for the management tool is often associated with the reinventing government movement of the 1990s that encouraged local governments to steer the boat in addition to rowing it (Osborne & Gaebler, 1992). The importance of performance measurement is that it requires public officials to move beyond financial accountability with budget documents and financial reports and requires them to embrace operational accountability through output, efficiency, and outcome measures. In other words, public officials have historically relied on budget-to-actual variance reports, for example, to demonstrate that they have remained within their appropriation limits. Performance measurement moves beyond the tracking of line-item variances and requires practitioners to collect and report information on the quantity of services provided (number of building inspections), the cost per service unit provided (cost per building inspection), and the quality of service provided (building inspections completed within 24 hours of request) to the citizens within their respective communities.

More recently, there has been a paradigm shift with regard to the study and practice of measuring the various dimensions of service delivery, where the focus has moved from performance measurement to performance management. Moynihan (2008) described performance management as the shift beyond collecting and reporting performance data to actually analyzing and using them for making management decisions. In other words, there is some value regarding accountability and transparency when reporting on the outputs, efficiencies, and outcomes of service delivery. The greater return on investment from well-managed performance measurement systems, however, is when public officials use performance measures to support changes in service delivery. These same measures are then used to track the success of these management decisions in terms of enhanced service efficiency and effectiveness over time, including the change in resources consumed for service provision. The difficulty in performance management, as shown by prior research, is that public officials often struggle with making the shift from measurement to management. Part of this struggle comes from the reality that different organizational characteristics like the need for top-down and bottom-up leadership are required for analyzing and using performance measures for making management decisions (Rivenbark, Fasiello, & Adamo, 2016).

Ammons and Rivenbark (2008) identified a number of organizational characteristics that increase the probability of public organizations engaging in performance management beyond leadership, including the utility of benchmarking and the reliance on efficiency measures. Benchmarking occurs when public officials analyze performance measures within the context of performance measures from other public organizations. In other words, the openness to compare one's performance against the performance of another actually increases the probability that public organizations will embrace performance management. Ammons and Rivenbark (2008) also found that public organizations engaged in benchmarking are particularly interested in the comparison of efficiency measures for making changes to service delivery within the context of performance management. The difficulty is making sure that efficiency measures are comparable from one organization to another given that they are calculated with the ratio of cost per service unit provided. More specifically, a robust methodology is needed to ensure that the numerator of total cost of service delivery and the denominator of total service units are calculated correctly before an accurate, reliable, and comparable efficiency ratio can be used for benchmarking consortiums, which can be challenging with public goods and services.

This chapter presents the intrinsic value of cost accounting in calculating comparable efficiency measures for the management tool of benchmarking and for the paradigm shift from performance measurement to management in public organizations. It begins with an overview of the three types of benchmarking before presenting the North Carolina Benchmarking Project, which has been in existence for 20 years and which has relied on a robust cost accounting methodology for reporting accurate, reliable, and comparable efficiency measures across multiple service providers. This methodology includes the calculation of direct, indirect, and capital costs for determining the organizational resources consumed for each of the 13 functional areas currently contained in the benchmarking report (Roenigk, 2015). It then presents information on why local governments participate in the benchmarking consortium and includes two case studies on how efficiency measures have been used to advance performance management within the service areas of residential refuse collection and fleet services. This chapter concludes with several observations on the challenges of implementing and managing cost accounting systems for the calculation of efficiency measures and on the future of benchmarking both from a theoretical and practical perspective.

Benchmarking

Ammons and Roenigk (2014), in responding to scholars who have questioned the value of benchmarking in the public sector, suggested that the problem is not with benchmarking but rather how it is being conceptualized both in theory and practice. The authors maintained that the barrier to benchmarking is the tendency for researchers to approach the management tool as a general concept rather than assessing each form of benchmarking based on its own merits. Overcoming this barrier, as described by Ammons and Roenigk (20014), has the possibility of advancing the theory and practice of benchmarking; therefore, this section begins with information on the different types of benchmarking to avoid presenting the North Carolina Benchmarking Project as a general concept rather than a specific type of the management tool.

Types of Benchmarking

There are three types of benchmarking approaches in the public sector, including corporate-style benchmarking, targets as benchmarks, and comparison of performance statistics as benchmarks (Ammons, 2000). Each, of course, contains strengths and weaknesses. The common thread that runs through the three types is the process of identifying a benchmark in order to provide context for analyzing one's current performance with the goal of implementing changes when a performance gap exists between the two data points. There also are some fundamental differences between the three types that public officials need to understand before investing the time and energy it takes to successfully implement any type of benchmarking initiative. In other words, understanding the strengths and weaknesses of any management tool is essential for realizing an adequate return on investment.

Corporate-style benchmarking, as the name implies, was adopted from the private sector. It involves the process of an organization specifically seeking to identify and implement "the" best practice of service delivery. There are three critical steps within the process of corporate-style benchmarking that create challenges for successful implementation in the public sector. The first is for the public organization to determine a very specific process to benchmark. While processes can be easily identified and mapped in the private sector for the production of goods, it is more challenging to diagram specific service delivery processes in the public sector, especially when there are multiple functional areas involved. The second step is for the public organization to identify another organization known for its best-in-class service delivery approach in order to establish benchmarks and to seek best practices. This step is the reason for why corporate-style benchmarking is not as common in the public sector compared to the other two forms of benchmarking. The third step is for the public organization to contact the best-in-class organization for obtaining information on establishing appropriate benchmarks and on best practices being used for service delivery, with the goal of implementing these best practices for closing the performance gap. The strength of corporate-style benchmarking is the establishment of benchmarks from organizations known as best-in-class and the ability to identify best practices of service delivery from these same organizations. In other words, corporate-style benchmarking is a prescriptive tool (Ammons, 2000). The challenge with this form of benchmarking is with locating service providers known as best-in-class for establishing benchmarks and with adapting, rather than adopting, best practices in response to current politics, organizational capacity, and stakeholder demands (Ammons, 1999)

Targets as benchmarks is the most difficult to describe among the three types of benchmarking because this type of benchmarking is aimed more toward closing performance gaps of societal outcomes rather than toward internal processes (Kelly & Rivenbark, 2011). For example, the state of Oregon initiated a strategic planning process in the 1990s, known as Oregon Shines, as to make progress toward the three major goals of quality jobs, community safety, and sustainable surroundings (Kissler, Fore, Jacobson, Kittredge, & Steward, 1998). The state identified and tracked numerous benchmarks for societal outcomes as part of this process. For example, benchmarks were established for indicators like unemployment, crime rates, high school graduation rates, and poverty rates and strategies were identified and funded by the legislature in an attempt to close the performance gaps between the actual indicators and the benchmarks over a 20-year period. A clear advantage to this form of benchmarking is the shift from internal processes of service delivery to external outcomes that impact the overall quality of life within the respective communities of the state. However, there are two main challenges to this form of benchmarking. The first is how the benchmark is actually established, where the ultimate target is often driven by desire rather than actual trends from external sources. The second is many of these societal outcomes are driven by forces outside the control of public organizations. Therefore, it can be difficult to understand the actual cause-and-effect relationships between policy changes and actual outcomes.

Comparison of Performance Statistics as Benchmarks is the most popular form of benchmarking, especially among local governments. This form of benchmarking, which is often managed by a third party, follows the process of collecting performance and cost data from participating local governments on an annual basis across multiple functional areas; calculating the output, efficiency, and effectiveness measures associated with each functional area; and reporting them in a format that shows how a local government's performance indicators compare against the other service providers. The ICMA started a national benchmarking consortium in 1994 (Coe, 1999), which falls into the category of comparison of performance statistics as benchmarks, and continues to manage and expand the consortium today. The benefit of this form of benchmarking is the amount of performance and cost data collected from each local government on an annual basis and the number of performance indicators that are published across multiple functional areas like environmental services, public safety, parks and recreation, and enterprise services. This provides local governments with a wealth of information on determining where the performance gaps exist within their organization as determined by comparisons from other local governments.

There are two fundamental challenges that local governments must understand before joining a benchmarking consortium that falls within the category of comparison of performance statistics as benchmarks. First, the local government must be willing to invest time in collecting, cleaning, and reporting the data in conjunction with the third party that manages the overall consortium. In other words, there is an inherent challenge in reporting accurate, reliable, and comparable performance measures across multiple public organizations (Rivenbark & Pizzarella, 2002). The second is that this type of benchmarking is diagnostic (Ammons, 2000), which requires a local government to move in the direction of corporate-style benchmarking in order to close the performance gap. While the local government is not seeking best in class, it must contact the high-performing organizations as revealed by a selected performance indicator and to determine the practices they are using for service delivery. The local government also must identify whether or not these practices can be adapted to its current organizational environment.

North Carolina Benchmarking Project

The impetus of the North Carolina Benchmarking Project came from two groups. The North Carolina League of Municipalities held a meeting for local government managers in 1994 to focus on issues related to privatization, which also led to a discussion on the need for reliable performance and cost data for the purpose of comparison. During this same period, the budget director of the city of Winston-Salem, North Carolina, at the annual conference of the North Carolina Local Government Budgeting Association, made a proposal to the membership to start some form of benchmarking consortium in order to analyze internal performance measures within the context of other service providers. These conversations ultimately resulted in the creation of the North Carolina Benchmarking Project in 1995, which is managed by the School of Government at the University of North Carolina at Chapel Hill (Rivenbark, 2001).

The North Carolina Benchmarking Project, which falls into the category of comparison of performance statistics as benchmarks, has been in existence for 20 years and continues to publish comparable performance and cost data on an annual basis. It also enjoys the primary advantage of this form of benchmarking, which is the amount of information that can be collected and reported on an annual basis. The *Final Report on City Service for Fiscal Year 2013–2014* contains over 150 performance measures, for example, across 13 functional areas from 13 municipalities. The functional areas include residential refuse collection, household recycling, yard waste/ leaf collection, police services, emergency communications, asphalt maintenance and repair, fires services, building inspections, fleet maintenance, central human resources, water services, wastewater services, and core parks and recreation (Roenigk, 2015).

It also must overcome the two major challenges associated with this type of benchmarking, including the inherent challenge of reporting accurate, reliable, and comparable performance measures across multiple public organizations and the reality that this form of benchmarking is diagnostic rather than prescriptive. This section of the chapter covers the annual data collection and reporting process and the cost accounting methodology used by the North Carolina Benchmarking Project to overcome the first challenge, including how efficiency measures are calculated given their importance in increasing the probability of local officials actually using performance data for decision making. The following section then covers why local governments in North Carolina continue to participate in the benchmarking consortium, including how they move from diagnostic to prescriptive information for improving the performance of service delivery.

Data Collection and Reporting

One of the advantages of a state-level benchmarking initiative like the North Carolina Benchmarking Project as compared to a national-level benchmarking initiative like the ICMA Benchmarking Consortium is that there is less variation in laws, policies, and services across the participating local governments. For example, all local governments in North Carolina are required by law to operate on a fiscal year beginning July 1. Therefore, the annual process of the North Carolina Benchmarking Project begins in July with a steering committee meeting, which is held in conjunction at the annual summer conference of the North Carolina Local Government Budget Association (the steering committee is composed of one employee from each participating jurisdiction). The purpose of the meeting is to review the process from the previous fiscal year, make adjustments to existing services under study, and discuss the possibility of adding new services to the project, which requires another separate process with the managers from the selected new service area to identify the service definition and the respective performance measures. Another key component of the meeting is to review the service delivery and cost accounting forms used to collect the needed performance and cost data for calculating the resource, workload, efficiency, and effectiveness measures associated with each service area from each of the 13 local governments currently participating in the project.

The School of Government then sends the updated service delivery and cost accounting forms to the respective local governments in August for completion by October, with the performance and cost data being based on the prior fiscal year. There is a separate service delivery form for each service area under study because of the variation in performance data required for each local government service. The service delivery form for household recycling collects data, for example, on collection points, set-out rates, tons collected, percentage of waste stream diverted from landfill, percentage of service contracted, and full-time equivalent (FTE) positions, while the service delivery form for water services collects data on average daily demand for water, operating treatment plants, miles of water main lines, number of water meters, and FTE positions. These specialized forms are completed by the respective service managers with the assistance of the local government employee who serves on the steering committee of the project. In addition to the individualized service delivery form, the standardized cost accounting form as shown in the Appendix is completed for each service area for calculating the total cost of service area. In other words, the form is used to capture the total organizational resources consumed for the delivery of a defined service area.

Each local government submits its completed forms to the School of Government in October. The project director enters the data into a central database (Excel) and calculates the respective performance measures for each service area. The project director also is responsible for cleaning the data, which involves comparing the calculated measures for reasonableness, comparing them to the prior fiscal year, and comparing them against each other for identifying possible outliers. The project manager is in constant contact with the steering committee members of the project, making the necessary adjustments for eliminating as many errors as possible. As discussed previously, the challenge to this form of benchmarking is the enormous amount of energy needed to collect, clean, and report performance and cost data that are accurate, reliable, and comparable. The project director distributes a draft report in January for another round of data cleaning. Once final changes have been made, the project director publishes the final report in February. This timeline is critical because local governments in North Carolina normally begin their annual budget preparation and enactment processes in January or February given that the new fiscal year begins July 1. Therefore, local governments have access to these benchmarking data for incorporating them into their annual budget processes, allowing them to move in the direction of performance budgeting (Kelly & Rivenbark, 2011).

Cost Accounting Methodology

Shortly after the North Carolina Benchmarking Project was created in 1995, steering committee members began to confront the difficulties with measuring the total cost of a defined functional area across multiple jurisdictions. The starting point was to compare the personnel and operating expenditures from the general ledger for each service delivery area under study. This information would then be used, for example, to calculate the cost per collection point for residential refuse collection, responding to the importance of this efficiency measure to solid waste directors. However, there are challenges with using only personnel and operating expenditures from the general ledger with a benchmarking consortium that falls into the category of comparison of performance statistics as benchmarks.

First, the operating expenditures are not going to be the same from one municipality to another. Some municipalities account for their fleet service activities, for example, within an internal service fund. A functional area like residential refuse collection that uses this internal service, as a result, will incur a direct change to one of its operating accounts for fleet maintenance. Other municipalities account for their fleet service activities within the general fund; therefore, functional areas like residential refuse collection are not charged directly for these services. The steering committee members quickly realized that these accounting differences would have to be reconciled for calculating comparable efficiency measures. Second, only comparing personnel and operating expenditures from the general ledger even when accounting differences were not an issue would not capture the capital costs of service areas. Capital costs for a service area like residential refuse are significant because of the high cost of acquiring the rolling stock units (garbage trucks) needed to collect refuse and the depreciation of these vehicles over time.

The steering committee finally decided to adopt a cost accounting methodology to capture the direct, indirect, and capital costs associated with each service area under study (Rivenbark & Carter, 2000). Again, the Appendix shows the cost form currently used by the North Carolina Benchmarking Project. While this form is completed for each service area under study, not all line items are completed for each service area given the variation in costs across different functional areas. For example, one of the line items under Section I is used to capture supplemental retirement income for law enforcement personnel, which would only be completed by the functional area of police services.

There is an individualized form for each functional area to capture the performance data as mentioned previously, and these forms are completed by the service manager in conjunction with the employee who serves on the project's steering committee. The standardized cost form, which must be completed for each functional area to determine the total organizational resources consumed by the respective service areas during the prior fiscal year, is normally completed by the finance director in conjunction with the employee who serves on the project's steering committee. There is another reason for collecting cost data at this level of detail beyond the desire of comparability of efficiency measures across the participating local governments. This level of detail also allows functional areas subject to privatization to monitor its cost in a form aligned with the private sector, which often reveals that the public sector can provide services more efficiently than the private sector.

The *direct costs* of each service area are captured in sections one and two of the cost form, representing the personal services and operating expenses.

While these data are normally taken directly from the general ledger, they must adhere to the definitions provided on the cost form, and adjustments may be still required for alignment with the service definition. The first major adjustment is often with personal services. It is common for solid waste employees to work in multiple functional areas, working in the functional area of residential refuse collection three days a week and working in the functional area of household recycling two days a week. This requires their total salaries and wages, including all benefits, to be split between two different cost forms. These adjustments may require the finance director to move beyond the general ledger and to obtain these data directly from the payroll ledger. Fortunately, some of the participating local governments use automated time systems that can track hours worked based on functional area, decreasing the amount of manual work needed for these calculations.

The second major adjustment is with the operating expenses, which has already been discussed. Some local governments use internal service funds for fleet services, for example. Therefore, this cost can be either a direct cost that is captured in Section II of the form or an indirect cost that is captured in Section III of the form. The issue is not where the cost is captured on the cost form because these line items are aggregated for the final report to show the total cost of service delivery. The issue is to make sure that each participating local government accounts for fleet services, for example, before returning the cost forms to the School of Government.

The *indirect costs* of each service area are captured in Section III of the cost form as shown in the Appendix. Indirect costs primarily represent the resources consumed by the functional area from support services. For example, the functional area of residential refuse collection relies on the functional area of human resources, which is accounted for in the general fund, for the recruiting and hiring of employees. A basis of allocation is needed, as a result, to determine the amount of organizational resources consumed from human resources by the functional area of residential refuse collection. Section III of the cost form shows that the basis of allocation for the human resources is the number of budgeted FTE positions. More specifically, the number of FTE positions budgeted for residential refuse collection is divided by the number of FTE positions budgeting for the municipalities. The resulting percentage is then multiplied by the total costs of human resources to determine the amount that can be contributed to the functional area of residential refuse collection.

However, participating local governments have the flexibility to use other methodologies for capturing indirect costs. Another in-house methodology would be to divide the number of recruitments for residential refuse collection by the total number of recruitments for the municipality to determine the respective percentage. Participating local governments also often hire consultants to prepare indirect cost plans, which they can use for participating in the North Carolina Benchmarking Project and for other possibilities like grant applications. Similar to the discussion on direct costs, the issue is to make sure that each participating local government accounts for its indirect cost regardless of methodology before returning the cost forms to the School of Government. This was determined after several rounds of collecting cost data across multiple local governments, where total cost was impacted by omitting particular indirect cost items rather than the indirect cost methodology selected for calculation.

The *capital costs* of each service area are captured in Section IV of the cost form, representing the depreciation of equipment and vehicles and the depreciation of buildings and infrastructure. The capital cost associated with each functional area also represents one of the primary reasons that the original steering committee decided on using a cost accounting methodology for capturing the total cost for each service area under study. It quickly became apparent that some local governments use pay-as-you-go financing for acquiring capital assets used for service delivery, which represents a cash outlay during the fiscal year of acquisition and which can skew the cost of service delivery. Other local governments, however, use debt financing for acquiring these same capital assets, which results in debt payments over the life of the loan and which also can skew the cost of service delivery.

In order to prevent financial policy decisions from impacting the efficiency of service delivery, the steering committee decided to adopt a depreciation schedule to capture the capital cost for each functional area. For example, maintenance equipment that exceeds the organization's capitalization threshold is depreciated at a rate of 12% while automobiles and light vehicles are depreciated at a rate of 30% on shown in Section IV of the cost form. An unforeseen benefit that resulted from the adoption of this methodology is that local governments had to spend resources on cleaning and maintaining accurate lists of capital assets assigned to each functional area, which also decreases the probability of local governments receiving a qualified audit opinion from their auditors during the annual audit of their financial statements.

Ammons and Rivenbark (2008), as mentioned previously, found that public organizations engaged in benchmarking are particularly interested in the comparison of efficiency measures for making changes to service delivery within the context of performance management. Therefore, the accuracy of the individual line items located on the cost form is critical to calculating accurate, reliable, and comparable efficiency measures. Once all the service delivery and cost forms are forwarded to the School of Government, the project director enters the data in an Excel spreadsheet for calculating the respective performance measures. As for the efficiency measures, the individual line items on the cost form are aggregated to determine the total cost of service delivery. This aggregated number then becomes the numerator of the efficiency measures.

The primary output for each functional area is then selected as the denominator before making the efficiency calculation. The primary output for building inspections, for example, is the total number of inspections by type, including building, electrical, mechanical, and plumbing. The resulting efficiency measure is the cost per building inspection, which is tracked over a 5-year period for each local government. The efficiency measure also is benchmarked against the overall average of cost per building inspection from the local governments that actually participate in this service area over the same 5-year period (not all local governments provide this service). Therefore, each local government can monitor its efficiency over time through trend analysis and can monitor its efficiency against the project average through the context of benchmarking.

Accountability and Performance Management

Rivenbark, Roenigk, and Fasiello (in press) surveyed the local governments participating in the North Carolina Benchmarking Project for the *Final Report on City Services for Fiscal Year 2013–2014* (Roenigk, 2015), seeking lessons learned after 20 years of benchmarking. One of the primary reasons for pursuing this research was to understand why local governments participate in benchmarking consortiums that fall into the category of comparison of performance statistics as benchmarks and how they make decisions regarding the comparative data. The top reason for participating in the benchmarking project was greater internal accountability rather than the specific reason of performance management.

This outcome, however, should not be surprising given that this type of benchmarking technique is diagnostic, providing local governments with performance information on departmental accountability over time and within the context of other service providers. Therefore, the second part of the research question focused on how local governments review and make decisions regarding the comparative data. Local governments responded that they tend to use the information for establishing service delivery goals and for publishing key results in the annual budget document when their performance measures are ranked at or above the overall average. This response would suggest that departments are satisficing to some degree, with the desire to be good enough within the context of existing resources (Davis, 1998).

The responses were very different, however, when departmental rankings were low as compared to the other service providers. First, the low performer analyzes the performance and cost data to ensure that data discrepancies are not causing the performance gap, returning to the importance of the data-cleaning process that occurs on an annual basis. Second, the low performer reviews the service processes used by the top performers in order to determine if they can be adapted for process improvement, which follows the approach of adapting rather than adopting as described by Ammons (1999). Therefore, local governments do use the information for performance management under certain circumstance, especially when performance gaps are identified with efficiency measures (Ammons & Rivenbark, 2008).

The following two case studies are included to demonstrate how local governments have embraced performance management. The first case is where the city of Concord, North Carolina, used the cost accounting methodology for performance management within the functional area of residential refuse collection and where a decision was made based on the analysis of service efficiency to renegotiate a contractual agreement (Rivenbark, Ammons, & Roenigk, 2005). The second case also is from the city of Concord, where maintenance costs per mile traveled were used to justify service delivery changes within the functional area of fleet services (Rivenbark, Ammons, & Roenigk, 2005). It should be noted, however, that local officials were proactive when moving from performance measurement to performance management in both of these cases, responding to the required additional analysis to use information from comparisons of performance statistics as benchmarks as a prescriptive tool. Building on this observation, Rivenbark, Roenigk, and Fasiello (in press) concluded their research that more examples are needed on how local governments actually use performance and cost data for decision making to assist practitioners with moving from measurement to management in public organizations.

Residential Refuse Collection[1]

Concord's solid waste staff began research in summer 2002 to determine if the city's five-year refuse and recycling collection contract with a private hauler should be renewed or if the city should bring collection back in-house. Benchmarking data from the *Final Report on City Services for Fiscal Year 2000–2001* indicated that Concord's cost per collection point was above the municipal average and that Concord had the highest number of complaints per 1,000 collection points. Although the cost measure decreased to $86 per collection point for fiscal year (FY) 2000–2001, which was more aligned with the municipal average, it was uncertain whether this represented a real trend or a onetime fluctuation.

Concord conducted an analysis using the North Carolina Benchmarking Project's full-cost accounting model. The analysis was completed in 2002 and was designed to determine whether a financial case could be made to bring refuse collection and recycling in-house. The city examined two equipment and personnel scenarios against the anticipated private hauler's contract cost. One scenario assumed a "low automation" design while the other scenario assumed a "high automation" design. The results of the analysis indicated that first-year start-up costs would exceed the expected private hauler cost but that over 5 years, the city would save between $700,000 and $1.1 million by operating the collection in-house. Determination of the potential quality improvement proved much more difficult to quantify. City staff felt confident that the mere element of having direct supervision over collection crews would result in a significant improvement in quality and overall responsiveness to daily collection problems raised by residents.

After the analysis was completed in 2002, city staff recommended to the city council at a January 2003 planning session to provide the collection service in-house or to renegotiate the hauling contract on a 2-year basis. The city council directed the city manager to remain with the private hauler but to renegotiate for a short-term contract (2 years instead of 5) and to put the hauler on notice that the city was serious about service improvement. The analysis and benchmarking data also were used as a tool in negotiating better rates and quality with the hauler. In light of the short-term contract renewal and a desire to confirm the original analysis, the city partnered with the School of Government's benchmarking staff members for a second analysis. The second analysis, completed in 2003, examined only "new" or additional costs to the city if collection were brought in-house. Results of the second analysis revealed similar findings as the first. After careful review, staff recommended in January 2004 that the city remain with the current hauler due to implementation challenges and "ramp up" timing concerns. The fact that service quality showed trends of improvement also presented an encouraging argument to remain with the private hauler. The city engaged the private hauler in a process to negotiate another new contract, using the benchmarking data to strengthen the city's negotiating position.

Once the private hauler understood that the city was seriously considering bringing residential refuse and recycling collection in-house, the hauler made noticeable improvement in service quality. Complaints per 1,000 collection points dropped by half, falling from 156 in FY 2000–2001 to 77 in FY 2003–2004. The city's latest collection contract specifies performance standards and a fine/incentive system for failure to meet basic service quality standards. Concord's latest collection contract requires monthly performance summaries and an annual customer satisfaction survey. Additionally, if the hauler's liquidated damages average does not exceed $750 per month and $1,500 total per quarter, damages are refunded to the hauler on a quarterly basis as an added incentive for good performance.

Concord's cost per collection point for residential refuse remains above the municipal average. However, the city has successfully negotiated lower rate increases by citing collection costs of other participants in the benchmarking project, especially those with in-house services. Initially, the contractor had proposed a rate of $7.76 per collection point per month. Based on the negotiations, the city was able to lower the beginning base cost to $7.07, a 9% drop. To this base amount, variable monthly fuel adjustments (not to exceed 4% per month) and annual CPI increases were added to determine each month's cost per collection point ($7.51 as of September 2005). While the cost in actual dollars per collection point has remained relatively flat for the last 5 years for Concord, the cost has declined when inflation is taken into account. Concord's cost per collection point has dropped from $98 in FY 1999–2000 to $87 in FY 2003–2004 when converted to 2000 constant dollars, which equates to an 11% reduction. The full-cost accounting model and the evaluation support from the School of Government provided

Concord a method to successfully influence the outcome of a contract negotiation process by accurately comparing in-house service delivery to private
service delivery. The benchmarking data also were instrumental in improving the quality of service provided to the citizens of Concord.

Fleet Maintenance

Performance and cost data for fleet services were collected and reported
for the first time in the *Final Report on City Services for FY 2001–2002*.
The comparative data for Concord revealed several potential problems,
including low shop productivity and excessive repeat repairs within thirty
days. Concord also discovered a high number of breakdowns during the
day, which affected the productivity in other departments as their equipment is not available for use. Consequently, problems in fleet maintenance
were increasing unscheduled maintenance work orders (breakdowns) and
decreasing the number of scheduled maintenance work orders (preventive
maintenance for brakes, tires, etc.). Scheduled maintenance work orders
are the most cost-effective, productive form of vehicle maintenance and
decrease the likelihood of costly breakdowns.

After analyzing the comparative benchmarking data, staff members
examined the operations of fleet maintenance in greater detail and found
multiple deficiencies. Fleet management was unaware of performance issues;
mechanics were provided little structure and given no expectations as to job
efficiency or shop productivity; fleet staffing structure was inefficient; many
fleet processes were inefficient (state inspections, preventive maintenance
procedures, scheduling and prioritizing work); the method of buying parts
increased downtime; warranty issues were not weighed against downtime; a
lack of communication between fleet maintenance and other city functions
increased repair costs; fleet software absorbed too much management time;
and vital scheduled maintenance was not being performed.

The most effective change was simply implementing accountability. Each
mechanic is now aware of performance standards and is provided a report
of individual and team productivity accomplishments on a monthly basis.
Not only do they see how they personally affect productivity, but they also
understand how and why the many process changes fleet maintenance has
implemented affect overall productivity. The process changes included the
creation of preventive maintenance check sheets (to ensure quality and promote accountability), the reduction of management staff by one FTE position, the implementation of state and federal inspection programs (saving
the cost of outsourcing and travel time), a change of purchasing practices to
promote competition, the use of multiple vendors to increase the likelihood
of completing repairs within 24 hours, the flagging of vehicles near retirement to reduce unnecessary maintenance, the reorganization of second shift
to focus on preventive maintenance as opposed to repairs, the creation of
trouble forms to expedite communication between first- and second-shift

supervisors, and the enforcement of preventive-operation checks, which decrease unscheduled maintenance work orders.

The operational changes helped reduce maintenance costs by three cents per vehicle-mile, from 18 cents in 2002 to 15 cents in 2005. This represents a savings of $120,000 over a 3-year period in Concord's fleet maintenance operations. The elimination of a management position also created an annual savings of approximately $45,000. Other improvements were documented as well. Hours billed as a percentage of billable hours increased from 53% in FY 2001–2002 to 70% in FY 2003–2004. The percentage of work orders completed within 24 hours increased from 81 percent to 86 percent, and the percentage of work orders requiring repeat repairs within 30 days decreased from 1.1 percent to 0.4 percent during the same period. Another area of improvement occurred in the replacement of transmissions. After the transmission preventive-maintenance program was implemented, the replacement of transmissions decreased from 24 in 2002 to 5 in 2005. A key to any successful performance measurement program begins with accurate and meaningful data. Effectiveness and efficiency measures are more useful than workload measures are, and Concord has found it beneficial to track these measures on a monthly basis as opposed to annually. Sharing performance information and getting buy-in from those actually doing the work also are crucial to a successful performance measurement program.

Conclusion

This chapter presented the intrinsic value of cost accounting for calculating comparable efficiency measures for the management tool of benchmarking. It began with an overview of the three types of benchmarking, which are corporate-style benchmarking, targets as benchmarks, and comparison of performance statistics as benchmarks. It then provided an overview of North Carolina Benchmarking Project, which has been in existence for 20 years and which has relied on a robust cost accounting methodology for calculating the direct, indirect, and capital cost of each functional area contained in the annual benchmarking report. The chapter then presented research on why local governments participate in North Carolina Benchmarking Project, which includes accountability and performance management. Two cases from the city of Concord, North Carolina also were included to specifically provide examples on how performance and cost data from a comparison of performance statistics as benchmarks project can be used as a prescriptive tool, in other words, to show how public officials moved from performance measurement to performance management of actually using data for decision making.

While there are numerous benefits to cost accounting as described in this text, there also are several challenges to implementing and managing cost accounting systems over time. The first is that financial management systems in public organizations are primarily designed to support fund accounting, which ultimately allows governmental organizations to produce an annual financial statement in accordance with generally accepted accounting principles (GAAP) as promulgated by the Governmental Accounting Standards Board (GASB). Therefore, local officials will need to invest additional resources in the technology for maintaining accounting systems with the flexibility of producing fund-level financial statements and producing functional-level cost data. In addition to this initial investment, public officials must be committed to implementing data on an ongoing basis that can be aggregated through the lens of an economic, financial, and cost perspective.

Another challenge is that public organizations will need to obtain the additional knowledge capacity to move in the direction of cost accounting. While public administrators and public accountants are often exposed to cost accounting during their degree course work, very few have the understanding of the actual practice of cost accounting in a governmental setting. Therefore, additional resources will be needed to acquire this capacity. In the case of the North Carolina Benchmarking Project, the participating municipalities pay an annual fee to the School of Government for a project director who manages the benchmarking consortium and who provides the necessary leadership for the cost accounting methodology described in this chapter. A final challenge of cost accounting in public organizations is determine how the data will be used to support decision-making processes. Given the amount of energy required to implement and manage cost accounting systems, public officials must understand how they will actually use the data for obtaining a return on investment. For the North Carolina Benchmarking Project, local governments clearly understand that the cost accounting methodology is used to produce accurate, reliable, and comparable efficiency measures and that these indicators are often used as the basis for performance management.

The primary purpose of this chapter is to describe the utility of cost accounting within the context of benchmarking, which raises the question of the future of benchmarking. There is interest in the management tool from both practitioners and scholars on a national and an international level (Ammons & Rivenbark, 2008; Ammons & Roenigk, 2014; Bovaird & Loffler, 2002; Kuhlmann, 2010; Walker & Andrews, 2015; Yasin, 2002). The future of benchmarking, from a practitioner point of view, depends on the ability of public organizations to actually use the comparative data for decision making given the amount of organizational resources needed to actively participate in a meaningful benchmarking consortium. In other words, the future of benchmarking faces the same challenges as internal performance measurement systems where the emphasis is now being placed on performance management. The future of benchmarking, from a scholarly point of view, is straight forward. Research, as described by Ammons and Roenigk (2014), must expand the limited theory on benchmarking within the various types of benchmarking—corporate-style benchmark, targets as benchmarks, and comparison of performance statistics as benchmarks—rather than the tendency to treat all forms of benchmarking as a general comparative tool.

Appendix

Table A.1 Cost Form of the North Carolina Benchmarking Project

---

Section I: Direct Cost for Personal Services and Definition

Salaries & wages—permanent	Gross earnings of permanent employees subject to FICA and retirement regulations
Temporary and part—time salaries & wages	Gross earnings of all employees subject to FICA but not retirement regulations
Overtime and holiday pay	Full-time permanent employees
Longevity	Gross earnings of longevity pay
Step allowance—law enforcement	Payments to law enforcement officers
Step allowance—other	Payments to step allowance made to other employees
Supplemental retirement income plan—law enforcement	Payments to supplemental retirement plan provided for law enforcement officers
Supplemental retirement income plan—others	Payments to supplemental retirement plan for other employees
FICA and social security	Unit's share of social security taxes on wages
Retirement contribution	Payments to state or own retirement fund for eligible employees
Hospital and medical insurance	Unit's share of employee medical and hospitalization insurance
Disability insurance	Unit's share of cost of disability insurance
Unemployment compensation contribution	Unit's cost for unemployment compensation on workers
Workers' compensation contribution	Cost of workers' compensation: self-insured, medical costs, and compensation for lost job time
Deferred compensation and 403K	Unit's contribution to employee deferred compensation plans
Other benefits	Cost of any other benefits not classified above

---

Section II: Direct Cost for Operating Expenses and Definition

---

Operating Supplies	Materials needed for program to carry out its tasks and functions
Purchases for resale/cost of goods sold	Cost of property or materials purchased for resale or cost of goods sold
Travel and training	Employee expenses for travel and training
Maintenance and repair	Services for maintenance and repair
Licenses and fees	Fees for recording deeds and employee permits
Advertising	All media
Uniform purchase and rental	Employee use
Dues/memberships/subscriptions	Includes technical publications
Telephone	Includes all direct costs for telecommunications
Utilities	Includes all direct costs for utility services
Technology	Includes internal and external technology services

Section II: Direct Cost for Operating Expenses and Definition

Professional or contracted services	Costs of specialized services
Contract administration	Costs of administering service contracts
Property and facility maintenance	Charges for property and facility maintenance
Fleet maintenance	Direct changes for feet maintenance
Fuel	Fuel costs for vehicles
Miscellaneous	Any expenses not included in other categories

Section III: Indirect Cost and Basis of Allocation

Manager's office	Number of budgeted FTE positions
Governing board	Number of budgeted FTE positions
Clerk	Number of budgeted FTE positions
Legal services	Time allocation by function
Human Resources	Number of budgeted FTE positions
Budget office	Number of budgeted FTE positions
Finance office	Number of accounting transactions
Revenue office	Percentage of revenue collected
Purchasing	Number of purchase orders
Risk management	Number of budgeted FTE positions
Liability insurance	Number of budgeted FTE positions
Property insurance	Percentage of premium
Vehicle and equipment insurance	Percentage of premium
Central support services	Number of requisitions
Traffic engineering	Percentage of staff time
Transportation planning	Number of direct assignments
Real estate management	Number of properties managed
Economic development	Percentage of staff time
Communication services	Number of calls taken
Planning services	Percentage of staff time
Departmental overhead—Personnel	Number of budgeted FTE positions
Departmental overhead—Operating	Number of budgeted FTE positions
Telephone	Communication instruments
Utilities	Square feet occupied
Technology	Number of service hours
Facility maintenance	Number of service hours
Fleet maintenance	Garage labor hours

Section IV: Capital Cost and Basis of Allocation

Furniture and office equipment	10 percent of acquisition cost
Maintenance equipment	12 percent of acquisition cost
Automobiles and light vehicles	30 percent of acquisition cost
Motor equipment	15 percent of acquisition cost
Data processing equipment	20 percent of acquisition cost
Miscellaneous equipment	10 percent of acquisition cost
Building	Based on 2 percent of original construction cost plus capitalized renovations and square footage occupied
Utility infrastructure	Based on 2 percent of original construction cost plus capitalized improvements

Note

1 The case studies on residential refuse collection and fleet maintenance were first reported in *Benchmarking for Results* (2005), a publication of the North Carolina Local Government Performance Measurement Project and the University of North Carolina School of Government. Reprinted with permission of the School of Government, copyright 2005. This copyrighted material may not be reproduced in whole or in part without the express written permission of the School of Government, CB# 3330 UNC Chapel Hill, Chapel Hill, North Carolina 27599–3330; telephone: 919–966–4119; fax 919–962–2707; Web: www. sog.unc.edu

References

Ammons, D. N. (1999). A proper mentality for benchmarking. *Public Administration Review*, *59*(2), 105–109.

Ammons, D. N. (2000). Benchmarking as a performance management tool: Experiences among municipalities in North Carolina. *Journal of Public Budgeting, Accounting & Financial Management*, *12*(1), 106–124.

Ammons, D. N., & Rivenbark, W. C. (2008). Factors influencing the use of performance data to improve municipal services: Evidence from the North Carolina benchmarking project. *Public Administration Review*, *68*(2), 304–318.

Ammons, D. N., & Roenigk, D. J. (2014). Benchmarking and interorganizational learning in local government. *Journal of Public Administration Research and Theory*, *25*(1), 309–335.

Bovaird, T., & Loffler, E. (2002). Moving from excellence models of local service delivery to benchmarking good local government. *International Review of Administrative Sciences*, *68*(1), 9–24.

Coe, C. (1999). Local government benchmarking: Lessons from two major multi-government efforts. *Public Administration Review*, *59*(2), 110–115.

Davis, P. (1998). The burgeoning of benchmarking in British local government. *Benchmarking for Quality Management & Technology*, *5*(4), 260–270.

Kelly, J. M., & Rivenbark, W. C. (2011). *Performance budgeting in state and local government*. Armonk, NY: M. E. Sharpe.

Kissler, G. R., Fore, K. N., Jacobson, W. S., Kittredge, W. P., & Steward, S. L. (1998). State strategic planning: Suggestions from the Oregon experience. *Public Administration Review*, *58*(4), 353–359.

Kuhlmann, S. (2010). Performance measurement in European local governments: A comparative analysis of reform experiences in Great Britain, France, Sweden, and Germany. *International Review of Administrative Sciences*, *76*(2), 331–345.

Moynihan, D. P. (2008). *The dynamics of performance management: Constructing information and reform*. Washington, DC: Georgetown University Press.

Osborne, D., & Gaebler, T. (1992). *Reinventing government*. New York: Penguin Group.

Rivenbark, W. C. (2001). *A guide to the North Carolina local government performance measurement project*. Chapel Hill, NC: Institute of Government.

Rivenbark, W. C., Ammons, D. N., & Roenigk, D. J. (2005). *Benchmarking for results*. Chapel Hill, NC: School of Government.

Rivenbark, W. C., & Carter, K. L. (2000). Benchmarking and cost accounting: The North Carolina approach. *Journal of Public Budgeting, Accounting & Financial Management*, *12*(1), 125–137.

Rivenbark, W. C., Fasiello, R., & Adamo, S. (2016). Moving beyond innovation diffusion in smaller local governments: Does performance management exist? *Public Administration Quarterly, 40*(4), 73–98.

Rivenbark, W. C., & Pizzarella, C. M. (2002). Auditing performance data in local government. *Public Performance & Management Review, 25*(4), 413–420.

Rivenbark, W. C., Roenigk, D. J., & Fasiello, R. (in press). Twenty years of benchmarking in North Carolina: Lessons learned from comparison of performance statistics as benchmarks. *Public Administration Quarterly, 40*(4), 763–788.

Roenigk, D. J. (2015). *Final report on city services for fiscal year 2013–2014.* Chapel Hill, NC: School of Government.

Walker, R. M., & Andrews, R. (2015). Local government management and performance: A review of the evidence. *Journal of Public Administration Research and Theory, 25*(1), 101–133.

Williams, D. W. (2003). Measuring government in the early twentieth century. *Public Administration Review, 63*(6), 643–659.

Yasin, M. M. (2002). The theory and practice of benchmarking: Then and now. *Benchmarking: An International Journal, 9*(3), 217–243.

4   Cost Accounting for Rates and User Fees

JoEllen Pope and Zachary T. Mohr

It is important to see why cost accounting is relevant to government rates, fees, and charges, which we collectively refer to in this chapter as user fees.[1] The main reason that it is important is that by not using cost accounting to account for overhead and indirect costs the total cost of the service is under-priced. This leads to several unintended problems and consequences such as overconsumption of the service by the consumer and lack of incentives to become more efficient in the use of overhead resources by the service provider. Additionally, when cost accounting is not used to figure the cost of a service that will be passed on to government customers, the service has to be financed with general tax resources. This puts a strain on the general budget and may be a burden to the citizens that pay the taxes when the service is provided to other people or businesses that live outside of the jurisdiction. Finally, different classes, or types, of customers may use the service at different times or in different amounts, which may change the cost of serving these customers. For these reasons, public finance has long advocated that user fees and charges be based on the cost to serve the consumer of the service (Musgrave, 1959).

Since the 1970s, local governments in the United States have relied more upon user fees to finance public services (Jung & Bae, 2011; Shadbegian, 1999). For example, Jung and Bae note that in 1972 the share of revenue for counties that came from user fees was 25.3% of own source revenues and increased to 42.4% by 2002. Calculations from the census of government show that in 1992 the share of revenue[2] that came from charges and utilities for state government was 9.8% and 32.4% for all local governments. By 2012, the share of charges and utilities revenue for state and local government had grown to 28.0% and 51.0%, respectively. This means that the percentage has almost tripled for state governments, and now local government is getting more than half of their non-intergovernmental revenue from user fees and related business-like activities.

The reason for this shift to more user fees is generally attributed to three reasons. The first is tax and expenditure limitations (TELs) that have severely limited local governments to raise tax revenue (Shadbegian, 1999). The second reason is the decline of federal and state grants to local governments, which peaked in the 1970s and declined quickly in the 1980s due to the end of general revenue sharing (Jung & Bae, 2011; Krane, Ebdon, & Bartle, 2004). The final reason noted in the literature is that the courts have limited the use of property tax because of its unequal distribution to finance local school systems (Krane et al., 2004). The final result for all levels of government is a much greater reliance on user fees and charges.[3]

While previous research has shown that cost accounting is empirically associated with the use of user fees and charges in both the federal government (Geiger & Ittner, 1996) and in local government (Mohr, 2015), descriptions about how they are being used and the key differences in cost accounting for user fees relative to other types of cost accounting such as grant cost accounting are absent from the general public administration and public accounting literatures. Important discussions for particular industry's specific cost accounting practices are available (see, for example, *Essentials of Cost Accounting for Health Care Organizations* by Finkler, Ward, and Baker or *Water and Wastewater Finance and Pricing* edited by Raftelis), but a discussion for general government is not to be found. To address some of the broader questions, this research asks two basic questions: First, how does cost accounting for user fees differ from other types of cost accounting? Second, what are some of the potential problems and additional considerations for user fees and rate setting? Because these are basic questions, this chapter is not an in-depth analysis of cost accounting for a particular industry, and it is not exhaustive of the cost accounting issues for user fees. It is suggestive of the broader points to consider for cost accounting for rates and fees and raises questions for considerations by managers and accountants that are trying to establish user fees based upon a cost of service.

The chapter is organized as follows: First, a discussion of the key features of cost accounting for user fees in a local government[4] context is provided with simplified examples of the calculations that are required. Next, we discuss some of the additional considerations concerning user fees for public services. Finally, we provide two cases of user fee problems to discuss some of the difficulties and ethical issues that surround cost accounting for the different types of user fees.

Key Features of Cost Accounting for Rate Setting

Determining costs for a utility is only one of the steps to setting reasonable user fees. Because costs are the primary way that courts and oversight bodies tend to adjudicate fees, it is a very important part of the user fee setting process. Before the cost allocations can be done, however, it is worth noting that the principles of the user fee structure should be discussed. For many services at the local level, such as water and sewer services, this is often simply that the service be provided in a sustainable and safe way. However, other considerations for the rate may also be relevant and are considered after the discussion of costs. The user-fee setter must also forecast demand

and usage levels and determine the revenue requirements for both operation and maintenance and capital expenditures. Then the costs must be allocated to the different classes of customers. Finally, the user fees for each class of customers must be set so that each class pays for its share of services. While each of these steps is worthy of discussion, it is the cost accounting step that is focused on here. The cost accounting and cost allocation are demonstrated in a simplified example to provide an illustration of the difference of cost accounting for setting user fees.

Overview of Cost Accounting for User Fees

The cost accounting process for user fees is often more complicated and involves more allocations than cost accounting for grants or other purposes because the costs must be allocated out to different customer classes. The customers who should be considered are the different types of customers who use the public service or good in a way that is different from other customers and, thus, have a different effect on the cost structure of the service. In most cost accounting in government, the cost allocation process ends at the level of service, but in Figure 4.1 we show that cost accounting for user fees extends to the customer.

The process to determine cost consists of four steps. AFAD can be used as an acronym for the cost determination process. The following steps used in this process have been adapted from Woodcock's model of the cost determination process, which they label FAD (Woodcock, 2015, pp. 183–184). Here, we first show that, in practice, there is a first allocation that is also necessary to cover the cost of city overhead service expense. The allocation of entity overhead, along with the process of functionalizing the categories, allocating the total revenue requirements, and distributing to customer categories, is shown with the following AFAD acronym:

1 Allocate any city or county central supporting costs to the individual service department that is determining specific service costs. The central supporting costs at the county or city level include but are not limited to county or city manager, attorney, information technology, finance, shared equipment or buildings, and clerk. This is the total revenue that is required for the cost of the utility.
2 Functionalize costs according to the various functions of the service. Using an example of water systems of a county or city, the functions include but are not limited to supply, treatment, storage, distribution, hydrants, meter, billing, and collection.
3 Allocate costs to different types of cost categories. For water systems of a county or city, the cost categories include but are not limited to baseline conditions, peak use, billing costs, and fire protection.

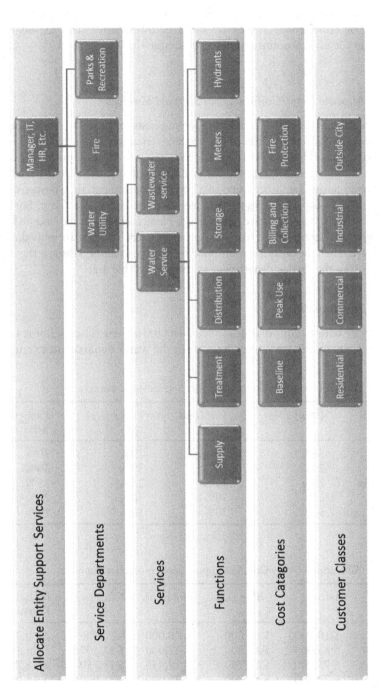

Figure 4.1 Hierarchy of Costs to Be Allocated and Distributed

4 Distribute the costs to different customer classes. The different classes of customers can be grouped together by use such as residential, industrial, or commercial and/or by other characteristics such as location within the city or county limits and outside the legal boundary.

Step 1—Allocate City-/County-Level Support Services

First, allocation of the city or county supporting costs to the service departments is necessary. Not all cities and counties are large enough to have dedicated support services for each department. In addition, there are certain positions, such as city or county manager, that are rarely duplicated at the service department level. If costs cannot be directly tied to a specific department, then costs can be allocated based on percentages derived from a meaningful cost driver. For the example, water service costs are determined. First, percentages are assigned for each supporting service cost to each city or county service department as shown in Table 4.1. Then the costs are multiplied by each percentage to assign the supporting cost to the service department as shown in Table 4.2.

Step 2—Functionalize Costs

After city or county supporting service costs have been allocated, it is time to assign costs to department functions. In the water department example,

Table 4.1 Allocation of City/County Support Service—Percentages

Costs	Utility Dept.	Fire Dept.	Police Dept.	Parks & Recreation
Manager	30%	20%	20%	30%
Attorney	20%	20%	30%	30%
Accounting	25%	25%	25%	25%
HR	20%	30%	30%	20%
IT	30%	30%	30%	10%

Table 4.2 Allocation of City/County Support Service—Dollar Amounts

Costs	Amount	Utility Dept.	Fire Dept.	Police Dept.	Parks & Recreation
Manager	$ 100,000	$ 30,000	$ 20,000	$ 20,000	$ 30,000
Attorney	$ 85,000	$ 17,000	$ 17,000	$ 25,500	$ 25,500
Accounting	$ 75,000	$ 18,750	$ 18,750	$ 18,750	$ 18,750
HR	$ 70,000	$ 14,000	$ 21,000	$ 21,000	$ 14,000
IT	$ 70,000	$ 21,000	$ 21,000	$ 21,000	$ 7,000
	$ 400,000	$ 100,750	$ 97,750	$ 106,250	$ 95,250

Table 4.3 Functionalized Water Costs—Percentages

Costs	Supply	Treat-ment	Storage	Distri-bution	Hyd-rants	Meters	Billing & Collection
Customer Service & Billing	0%	0%	0%	0%	0%	0%	100%
Utility Admini-stration	5%	5%	5%	5%	5%	15%	60%
Insurance	25%	15%	15%	15%	15%	10%	5%
Assigned Entity Supporting services	10%	10%	10%	20%	10%	20%	20%
Inspections	25%	50%	5%	10%	0%	10%	0%
Maintenance	30%	25%	5%	30%	5%	5%	0%

the functional categories for the department include supply, treatment, storage, distribution, hydrants, meter, billing, and collection. The functional allocation is done much the same as the entity supporting service allocation. The functions are identified for the particular service department then costs are assigned to the functions. Using the chart of accounts is a good way to identify costs to be allocated to each function. In addition, entity-supporting service costs that were allocated to the department should be allocated to each function. Again, if the cost cannot be directly tied to a function, percentages can be used to allocate the cost among the department functions. First, percentages for allocating costs to each function must be established as shown in Table 4.3. Then the percentages are applied to the actual or estimated costs to assign costs to each function as shown in Table 4.4.

Step 3—Allocate Costs to Categories

The next step in the cost determination process is to allocate functional costs to different cost categories. In the example for water service, the categories are baseline capacity, peak use, customer service, and fire protection. This step is performed similarly to the previous steps. Allocation percentages are established to allocate the functional costs to the costs categories as shown in Table 4.5. These percentages may be established using historical information about daily or hourly usage. In the case of the water department example, the functional expenses are allocated among the cost categories of base, peak use, customer service, and fire protection using the assigned percentages, as shown in Table 4.6. Usually, the allocation of costs between base and peak use is done because the peak use often costs significantly more than base capacity.

Table 4.4 Functionalized Water Costs—Dollar Amounts

Costs	Amounts	Supply	Treatment	Storage	Distribution	Hydrants	Meters	Billing & Collection
Customer Service & Billing	$ 200,000	$—	$—	$—	$—	$—	$—	$200,000
Utility Administration	$ 150,000	$ 7,500	$ 7,500	$ 7,500	$ 7,500	$ 7,500	$ 22,500	$ 90,000
Insurance	$ 75,000	$ 18,750	$ 11,250	$ 11,250	$ 11,250	$ 11,250	$ 7,500	$ 3,750
Assigned Entity Supporting services	$ 100,750	$ 10,075	$ 10,075	$ 10,075	$ 20,150	$ 10,075	$ 20,150	$ 20,150
Inspections	$ 100,000	$ 25,000	$ 50,000	$ 5,000	$ 10,000	$—	$ 10,000	$—
Maintenance	$ 100,000	$ 30,000	$ 25,000	$ 5,000	$ 30,000	$ 5,000	$ 5,000	$—
	$ 725,750	$ 91,325	$ 103,825	$ 38,825	$ 78,900	$ 33,825	$ 65,150	$313,900

Table 4.5 Allocation of Water Costs to Categories—Percentages

Functions	Base	Peak Use	Customer Service	Fire Protection
Supply	100%			
Treatment	65%	35%		
Storage	65%	35%		
Distribution	65%	35%		
Hydrants				100%
Meters			100%	
Billing & Collection			100%	

Table 4.6 Allocation of Water Costs to Categories—Dollar Amounts

Functions	Total Cost	Base	Peak Use	Customer Service	Fire Protection
Supply	$ 91,325	$ 91,325	$—	$—	$—
Treatment	$ 103,825	$ 67,486	$ 36,339	$—	$—
Storage	$ 38,825	$ 25,236	$ 13,589	$—	$—
Distribution	$ 78,900	$ 51,285	$ 27,615	$—	$—
Hydrants	$ 33,825	$—	$—	$—	$ 33,825
Meters	$ 65,150	$—	$—	$ 65,150	$—
Billing & Collection	$ 313,900	$—	$—	$ 313,900	$—
	$ 725,750	$ 235,333	$ 77,543	$ 379,050	$ 33,825

Step 4—Distribute Costs to Customer Classes

Once the functional costs have been allocated to the various cost categories, the next step in the cost determination process is to distribute these costs to the different customer classes. First, the total usage is determined for each cost category. Then the total cost allocation is divided by the number of units as show in Table 4.7. This is the per-unit cost for each category. Then the number of units used per customer class is determined. The cost per class is then allocated by the cost per unit multiplied by the number of units used by a particular class.

The final step is to set rates that will meet the objectives of the utilities rate setting process for each of the classes. Most often these rates are set to make the service sustainable, but there are also additional issues that must also be considered when setting the rate structure. These additional issues are discussed in the next section and will be powerfully influenced by the type of service, the community, and the purposes for which the service is intended.

Table 4.7 Distribution of Water Costs to Customer Classes

	Base	Peak Use	Customer Service	Fire Protection
Total Usage	125,233	1,333	75,000	N/A
Unit of Measure	kgal	kgal/day	Number of Contacts	N/A
Total Allocation	$ 235,333	$ 77,543	$ 379,050	$ 33,825
Unit Cost	$ 1.88	$ 58.17	$ 5.05	N/A
Classes				
Residential Units	75,139.80	799.80	45,000	
Costs	$ 141,199.50	$ 46,525.50	$ 227,430.00	
Commercial Units	25,046.60	266.60	15,000	
Costs	$ 47,066.50	$ 15,508.50	$ 75,810.00	
Industrial Units	12,523.30	133.30	7,500	
Costs	$ 23,533.25	$ 7,754.25	$ 37,905.00	
Outside City/ County Units	12,523.30	133.30	7,500	
Costs	$ 23,533.25	$ 7,754.25	$ 37,905.00	
Fire Protection				$ 33,825
Units	125,233	1,333	75,000	N/A
Costs	$ 235,333	$ 77,543	$ 379,050	$ 33,825

Additional Issues in Rate Setting

Neoclassical economic theory is unequivocal that pricing decisions should be based on the cost of producing a good or service. This is so because the price that is connected to the cost to produce the good or service sends a signal to the market that an expensive service is scarce and must be conserved. In this way, the fully functioning market economy is an important mechanism for the sustainability of scarce resources.

Unfortunately, typical government services are either public goods or monopolistic in nature, so they almost never operate in fully functioning markets. Therefore, the government service and the resulting cost determination differ markedly from for-profit firms. Profit is almost never the guide in determining the price of the service, and prices can be set without consideration of the full costs-of-service- provision as would be done in the private sector. In spite of the problems with public sector pricing, the ability to price a service may be an important policy tool to combat such things as traffic, resource scarcity, and pollution.

This section provides a guide to the ethical issues and other considerations that governments often must consider in pricing their services. This list is not exhaustive and is based in large part on the work of Carnegie and West (2010) and Carnegie, Tuck and West (2011), where they show that the simple formula for a government price is determined by the formula:

Price = Cost + Margin – Subsidy

The intuition of the formula is straightforward. Because a government does not always want to price its services at cost, it must either add a margin to the cost of the service or subtract a subsidy from the cost. The formula is useful for determining what may be an appropriate level of margin or subsidy. For example, the local government may want to charge a margin on services that it is providing to people who live outside its incorporated boundaries. These residents may choose to get services such as water, sewer, or trash from the community because they live relatively close, and the city can provide them at a much cheaper rate than these residents can get them from a private provider. Theoretically, the government is justified in adding an additional margin to the service because the nonresident is not an owner of the capital stock in the same way that the citizen is and, thus, does not share the risk. In these cases, adding a margin or return on the investment is appropriate and may be based upon some neutral rate such as the interest rate charged on treasury notes (Crea, 2015). As a practical matter, it is also important to charge a premium to the nonresident. Without a premium, there is no encouragement for incorporation of residents in the local jurisdiction because the nonresident can become a free rider on services that the government does not charge for, such as parks and roads, and is able to get the other necessary services at the same price as residents.

The subsidy is probably easier to understand because we often see public services that are highly subsidized when they have user fees attached to

Table 4.8 Additional Factors for Pricing Government Services

Financial Viability
Equity
Policy Levers
Accountability
Competition
Public Goods
Monopoly
Economic Development
Externalities and Congestion Pricing
Legal and Contractual
Political Factors

*Adapted from Carnegie and West (2010).

them. Governments often have many reasons for doing this such as equity, policy levers, and other political factors (See Table 4.8). Often governments subsidize services to senior citizens because the senior may live on a fixed income. This is a type of equity consideration that assumes that seniors have a lower ability to pay, and paying for services such as public transportation should not be excessively burdensome to people that have less ability to pay. Sensitive groups, such as senior citizens, may also be seen as politically important. Another reason that some services such as public transportation are subsidized is that they are important policy levers. In the case of public transportation subsidies, part of the justification for subsidizing the service is that it relieves congestion on the roads and reduces pollution.

Additionally, Carnegie and West note that factors like accountability and competition are important in the context of government. Unlike private businesses, governments often are required to be able to show how their prices are derived. Additionally, the expectation may be that the government does not compete with private businesses for the services that it provides, and when it does enter a competitive market, it is not supposed to engage in a noncompetitive pricing strategy. However, evidence shows that there are important cost accounting changes that can be made based upon the competitiveness of the market (Cavalluzzo, Ittner, & Larcker, 1998).

Carnegie and West note that characteristics of the market and service such as whether the service is truly a public good and whether the government is a monopoly provider influence the price of the service. If the good is truly a public good, then it is nonrivalrous and nonexcludable, which means that the government cannot stop people from consuming it. In practice, this means that public goods would be very hard to collect a fee from the users. Because pricing systems must themselves have a reasonable cost to collect the user fee, a service that is very difficult to collect may not be well suited for financing via a user fee. Additionally, monopolistic services provided by public entities are not disciplined by a market and, therefore, may have their prices based on something other than cost.

To Carnegie and West's list, which was in the context of Australian local governments, governments in the United States context use prices for a few other market-related purposes. First, local governments may give lower rates to industries as a form of economic development based on considerations of factors such as economies of scale or scope (Millonzi, 2010). Additionally, many types of public services must consider the capacity of the system to provide a service. To conserve the service at these peak times, congestion pricing theory suggests that governments should provide a surcharge for use during these peak times to limit strain on the system and to provide greater capacity (Downs, 2000).

Another important factor, which was implied in Carnegie and West's work but not addressed explicitly, is the legal issues that surround public service and the ability to charge for those services. The issues here are that governments may not be able to provide services, they may be contractually or legally bound not to charge for the service, or they may be contractu-ally or legally bound to only charge for the cost of the service. Especially for lower levels of government such as cities and counties, they may not be legally able to provide certain services. An example of such a service is state-run liquor stores. In some states, the state or the counties run the liquor stores, but in other states this is reserved only for the private market. If the government can legally provide the service, there are legal and contractual reasons that they cannot charge for it such as grant restrictions. Another legal example of not being able to charge for a service comes from the field of education, where many states have constitutional or legal restrictions that would prohibit charging for public education. Finally, even when a government has the ability to provide a service and charge for it, the higher levels of government or the people may determine or dictate the price that can be charged for it. For example, some states require municipal utilities to appear before or present their rates to the state utilities commission for approval. In California, Proposition 218 requires that all rates be based on cost, which may effectively eliminate the ability to use rates as policy levers or provide tiered rates for equity purposes. In all, the legal and con-tractual environment is an important aspect of rate setting for all levels of government.

Finally, Carnegie and West note that political factors are important in pricing services. They note that it is "inevitable" and "appropriate" that politics should inform the pricing decision but they also note that

> given this range of factors that are likely to exert influence, the pricing of local government goods and services is inevitably complex and multi-faceted. Yet, there are also legitimate demands for pricing decisions to be transparent and 'rational'. Therein lies the very substantial challenge of setting prices within the local government context.
>
> (Carnegie & West, 2010, p. 112)

Indeed, in the United States and throughout the world, rate setting can be a very real challenge. While it often aspires to a rational allocation based upon the full cost of service and balance of the forgoing practical and ethi-cal considerations, it can often lead to legal challenges in the courts (Wood-cock, 2015) and political scandals (Collier, 2006). As such, the following examples are provided which illustrate the difficulties of balancing the technical aspects of cost determination with the other ethical and practical considerations.

Case 1: City and Airport Fight Over Police Charges and the Politics of Control

The first case that we discuss shows the difficulty of establishing a charge that will not be contested in the public arena. The context is a large city in the United States that owns a hub airport of a large airline. The city and the airport have an extremely cost conscious culture and draw pride from keeping the cost of the airport low (Mohr & Mushipe, 2015). However, as the airport grew in size, it began to resent paying the administration and overhead charges that it was paying on its police services that it was forced to "buy" from the city. The questions about this case are whether the city was correct in applying overhead to the airport and what was the outcome of the airport's fight to free itself from the charges.

In this case, the city was correct that it should be charging overhead expenses to the police that the airport was using. The airport is large and had a large police presence. These police officers require additional work from human resources, payroll, and accounting, to name just a few of the administrative services that were being allocated to the cost of the police service. It would be a burden on the citizens to have to pay for these services that were largely being supplied to protect the traveling public that largely came from outside the jurisdiction. Based upon user pays principles, this was correct and the city documented and justified its rates with a transparent cost allocation plan (CAP) and methodology.

Eventually, the airport and state lawmakers began to reconsider the control of the airport and the charges that the city was making the airport pay. The state passed a law that stripped the city of its control of the airport and gave it to a regional governing body. Because the city owned the airport and had the license to operate the airport from the Federal Aviation Administration (FAA), the city appealed the ruling to the FAA. What followed was a protracted legal battle that eventually led the courts to leave the decision of control of the airport to the FAA. The FAA has not made a decision on this case. So, the city retains the license to operate the airport and the control that this gives the city. The city modified its CAP but still charges the airport for police service and the overhead consumed by the police.

This legal battle for control of the airport shows that cost accounting is important in politics and the running of institutions. At the very least, the cost accounting was an important issue in justifying stripping the city of its control of the airport. Unfortunately, political decisions are made at multiple levels and may not be concerned with technically or theoretically justifiable fees. In these cases, cost can become an extremely political issue.

Case 2: Lawsuits Over Water Prices in San Juan Capistrano, California

In the City of San Juan Capistrano in California, the city used a tiered rate structure based on the amount of water that was being consumed. The rate structure had four rate classes, and the rates that were charged increased based on increasing water usage. This principle is an important principle for discouraging excessive use in drought-stricken areas.

Eventually, the citizens sued the city over this policy because it violated Proposition 218. The city was forced to repay the citizens because the pricing of the water was not based on its cost (Cuniff, 2016). This ruling has important implications for all municipalities in the state, which may severely limit their ability to set rates that would encourage conservation (Cuniff, 2015). This case shows that the legal environment may trump the rates that the municipality tries to set. Even when a city does correct cost accounting and has a valid policy reason for applying a specific rate structure to a service, the courts or a regulatory body may step in to determine costs that are allocable.

Conclusion

While this chapter was a simple overview of the cost accounting necessary for rates and fees, it provides some context for the difficulty of establishing costs and rates for these fees. The cost that is allocated down to categories, such as peak usage, may vary based on the cost driver that is used, such as the difference between peak day or peak hour. These technical and difficult cost concepts may be further obscured by the number of ethical considerations that a community may want to make about the pricing of the services. Even though ethical and practical considerations about rates should influence the rate structure, it is important first to develop a good cost for each cost function and category so that appropriate financial and nonfinancial considerations can be made.

Notes

1 Rates, fees, and charges all have a similar meaning in this chapter. Even though they may be thought to be different, such that rates are usually applied to utilities and services like water and wastewater, fees are usually a service that is required but for which there is not an exchange transaction such as business licensing or planning and zoning reviews, and charges may be a charge for a service that is passed on to an internal customer of the organization, we classify them similarly here. The basic idea being that these are services for which there is some sort of charge that is being passed on to a customer either inside or outside the organization so that the service is able to recover its costs and be self-sustaining. Because we are using these terms synonymously for the purposes of the cost accounting, we simply refer to all three as user fees throughout the rest of the chapter.

2 Revenue = General Revenue – Intergovernmental Revenue and Transfers.

3 Even though the federal government is seeing increasing reliance on user fees. Although the federal government gets less than 10% of its revenue from user charges, the United States Government Accountability Office (2008) estimates that fees in the federal government increased from 1999 to 2007 in nominal dollars by 69%, or 39% after adjusting for inflation.

4 Principles of cost accounting for user fees for the federal government are in OMB Circular A-25.

References

Carnegie, G. D., Tuck, J., & West, B. (2011). Price setting practices in Australian local government. *Australian Accounting Review, 21*(2), 193–201.

Carnegie, G. D., & West, B. (2010). A conceptual analysis of price setting in Australian local government. *Australian Accounting Review, 20*(2), 110–120.

Cavalluzzo, K. S., Ittner, C. D., & Larcker, D. F. (1998). Competition, efficiency, and cost allocation in government agencies: Evidence on the Federal Reserve System. *Journal of Accounting Research, 36*(1), 1–32.

Collier, P. M. (2006). Costing police services: The politicization of accounting. *Critical Perspectives on Accounting, 17*(1), 57–86.

Crea, J. F. (2015). Identification of revenue requirements. In G. A. Raftelis (Ed.), *Water and wastewater finance and pricing* (pp. 149–180). Boca Raton, FL: CRC Press.

Cuniff, M. M. (2015, April 20). Court: San Juan Capistrano's tiered water rates are illegal, may hinder conservation. *Orange County Register.*

Cuniff, M. M. (2016, January 13). Lawsuit again San Juan Capistrano seeks millions in water-rate refunds. *Orange County Register.*

Downs, A. (2000). *Stuck in traffic: Coping with peak-hour traffic congestion.* Washington, DC: Brookings Institution Press.

Geiger, D. R., & Ittner, C. D. (1996). The influence of funding source and legislative requirements on government cost accounting practices. *Accounting, Organizations and Society, 21*(6), 549–567.

Jung, C., & Bae, S. (2011). Changing revenue and expenditure structure and the reliance on user charges and fees in American counties, 1972–2002. *The American Review of Public Administration, 41*(1), 92–110.

Krane, D., Ebdon, C., & Bartle, J. (2004). Devolution, fiscal federalism, and changing patterns of municipal revenues: The mismatch between theory and reality. *Journal of Public Administration Research and Theory, 14*(4), 513–533.

Millonzi, K. (2010). *CED in NC blog: Using utility rates as an economic development incentive tool.* Retrieved from https://www.sog.unc.edu/blogs/community-and-economic-development-ced/using-utility-rates-economic-development-incentive-tool

Mohr, Z. T. (2015). An analysis of the purposes of cost accounting in large US cities. *Public Budgeting and Finance, 35*(1), 95–115.

Mohr, Z. T., & Mushipe, T. (2015). *Beyond bean-counting: The role of costs during the Charlotte-Douglas Airport takeover.* Paper presented at the North Carolina Political Science Association, Charlotte, NC.

Musgrave, R. (1959). *The theory of public finance.* New York: McGraw-Hill.

Shadbegian, R. J. (1999). The effect of tax and expenditure limitations on the revenue structure of local government, 1962–87. *National Tax Journal, 52*(2), 221–237.

Woodcock, C. (2015). Determination of cost of service. In G. A. Raftelis (Ed.), *Water and wastewater finance and pricing* (pp. 183–203). Boca Raton, FL: CRC Press.

5 Cost Accounting for Government Grants

Robert J. Eger, III and
Bruce D. McDonald, III

This chapter is intended to identify and discuss the principles and norms for determining costs applicable to grants, contracts, and other agreements between the federal government and educational institutions, nonprofit organizations, and state, local, and Indian tribal governments. The Office of Management and Budget (OMB), together with the 26 federal awarding agencies, responded to President Obama's second-term management agenda and his first-term directives, under Executive Order No. 13520 and the objectives laid out by Mader (2014), to better target financial risks and better direct resources to achieve evidence-based outcomes. This executive order and the response from OMB do not include any new policy; however, they do include regulatory language required to streamline the existing voluminous body of agency regulations into alignment with the Uniform Guidance. This includes language eliminating more than 20 previously separate regulations in federal awards.

The regulatory goals are to unify the standards set out in three circulars that were published by the OMB. These are OMB Circulars A-21, A-122, and A-87, which guide cost principles and norms for federal grant accounting in educational institutions, nonprofit organizations, and state, local, and Indian tribal governments, respectively. The final guidance, which was originally published on December 26, 2013, as 78. Fed Reg. 78589, objectives are to simultaneously improve performance, transparency, and oversight for federal awards. The Council on Financial Assistance Reform (COFAR) will measure the impact of this guidance as described under M-14–17 (see Mader, 2014).

The joint interim final rule was issued to implement the new guidance as 2 CFR 200 (Uniform Guidance; *Uniform Administrative Requirements, Cost Principles, and Audit Requirements for Federal Awards*, 2013). Although uniformity and improvements in efficiency and effectiveness are the goals, the Uniform Guidance complexity has led affected organizations to focus on the prior OMB circulars. Given that these circulars are the underpinning of the Uniform Guidance and that cost principles under the Uniform Guidance have not been harmonized, this chapter identifies the cost accounting principles and norms based on the OMB circulars while offering potential future changes under the Uniform Guidance as they become implemented. Overall, the Uniform Guidance has minimal effects on the cost accounting principles and norms put forward in the OMB circulars. Although minimal effects are anticipated, readers should be aware that a potential effect lies with the timing and defining of a "new" award. The reader of this chapter must be aware of potential changes in timing and definition, and we try to articulate where potential changes may occur throughout this chapter. Currently Uniform Guidance is available through the Federal Register (see OMB, 2013).

We begin the chapter with an overview of cost accounting standards and provide definitions for each organizational type included in this chapter. Next we identify and define administrative, direct, and indirect costs as presented in both the OMB circulars and the Uniform Guidance. We then show how these costs are applied to each organizational type. We articulate the role of prudence and consistency as applied to the cost standards. We then explore the International Accounting Standards (IAS) for costs and show the application of these standards. We discuss and present examples as applied to organization type and then conclude with a discussion of the United States and international standards.

Cost Accounting Principles and Norms (CAPN)

Cost accounting principles and norms (CAPN) are the set of principles used for determining costs applicable to grants, contracts, and other agreements with the federal government. The norms deal with the subject of cost determination. The principles and norms are determined in accordance with generally accepted accounting principles (GAAP), except where restricted or prohibited by law, and are designed as an assurance that the federal government will bear its fair share of total costs.

The successful application of CAPN requires the development of a mutual understanding between representatives of grantee institutions and the federal government as to their scope, implementation, and interpretation of these costs. For this chapter, these principles and norms are a guide for agreements that are referred to as sponsored agreements, whether they are fixed price or lump-sum agreements. Sponsored agreements include research and development, training, and other sponsored work that are separately budgeted and accounted for by the grantee. This chapter focuses on three types of grantee organizations. These organizations are colleges and universities, nonprofit organizations, and state, local, and federally recognized Indian tribal governments. Although private for-profit (commercial) firms do receive federal funds through contracts, these organizations are not included in this chapter.

Defining Organizations

To perform sponsored work, OMB defines each type of organization within three separate circulars. These Circulars are the key to assurance that the organization is attentive to CAPN. The definition of the organizations varies from functional to descriptive. Attentiveness to the definition will allow any organization to understand its applicability of the CAPN for federally sponsored agreements.

Colleges and Universities

The first organization, colleges and universities, is defined in the OMB Circular A-21 (2004a). In Circular A-21, colleges and universities are defined as institutions whose major functions consist of instruction, organized research, other sponsored activities, and other institutional activities. Given that colleges and universities are defined based on their functions, Circular A-21 defines each function to provide guidance.

College and university instruction includes all teaching and training activities, whether they are offered for credits toward a degree or certificate or on a noncredit basis. These teaching and instruction activities can be offered through regular academic departments or separate divisions, such as university extensions.

Organized research for colleges and universities focuses on separately budgeted and accounted for research and development activities. Organized research is inclusive of sponsored research by federal and nonfederal organizations[1] along with research and development activities that are separately budgeted and accounted for under an internal application of institutional funds. The role of students engaged in research and the learning process, where the resulting benefits are to sponsored agreements, are considered in the application of these costs standards.

Other sponsored activities for colleges and universities are defined as programs and projects financed by federal and nonfederal organizations, which involve the performance of work other than instruction and organized research. The key aspect of the definitions for instruction, organized research, and other sponsored activities is the "support" aspect, which will require an application of the CAPN for allowable costs.

Other institutional activities that occur in colleges and universities are defined to include the operation of auxiliary enterprises. Importantly, any activities that are undertaken by the institution without outside support can be classified as other institutional activities. In general, other institutional activities are unallowable under sponsored agreements.

Nonprofits

In OMB Circular A-122 (2004b), nonprofits are defined as any corporation, trust, association, cooperative, or other organization which is operated primarily for scientific, educational, service, charitable, or similar purposes in the public interest. Central in this definition is that the nonprofit be aware that the descriptive definition contains two important caveats. Although these caveats are common to the definition of a nonprofit generally, awareness of the caveats is important. The caveats include that a nonprofit cannot be organized primarily for profit and that a nonprofit use its net proceeds to maintain, improve, and/or expand its operations. There are specific nonprofits that are excluded from coverage in Circular A-122 because of their size and the nature of their operations. These excluded nonprofits that operate under federal cost principles applicable to commercial organizations. Although these are few, some major nonprofits that are excluded are the Urban Institute and the RAND Corporation.

State, Local, and Federally Recognized Indian Tribal Governments

In OMB Circular A-87 (2004c) state, local, and federally recognized Indian tribal governments are defined in broad terms. A state includes all of the States of the United States, the District of Columbia, the Commonwealth of Puerto Rico, all territories or possessions of the United States, or all agencies or instrumentalities of the states.[2]

A local government includes any agency or instrumentality of a local government and any county, municipal government, city, town, or township. This broad definition of a local government is applied to local public authorities, school districts, special districts, intrastate districts, council of governments (whether or not incorporated as a nonprofit), and any other regional or interstate government entities.

Federally recognized Indian tribal governments are defined to include all entities certified by the secretary of the interior as eligible for the special programs and services provided through the Bureau of Indian Affairs. This includes all governing bodies or governmental agencies of any Indian tribe, band, nation, or other organized group or community.[3]

In all three OMB Circulars, the organizational definitions attempt to be both broad and specific to include all potential organizations that would need to follow the CAPN for federally sponsored agreements. This is identical to the goals found in the Uniform Guidance that is currently in the implementation process for sponsored agreements.

General Factors Affecting Allowable Costs

Prior to delving into the specific types of allowable costs that are used in CAPN, some guiding general factors are found in all three OMB Circulars. These general factors have an impact on the allowable costs under the CAPN and are mimicked in the implementation of the Uniform Guidance. Although in its implementation phase, the Uniform Guidance considers these factors in an attempt to reduce the reporting burden on all organizations receiving federally sponsored agreements. These factors help guide grantees toward the goal of efficient and effective sponsored agreement management.

Let us begin with the factors that affect the allowability of a cost in the three OMB Circulars. The first factor that is applied to an allowable cost is the notion of reasonableness. A reasonable cost is a cost that, in its nature or amount, does not exceed that which would be incurred by a prudent person under the circumstances prevailing at the time the decision was made to incur the costs. A simpler idea would be to think of the cost from a prudent person's point of view and say, "Is this cost reasonable?"

Next, an allowable cost must be determined in accordance with GAAP. This factor implies consistent treatment and allocability. Consistency and allocability are hallmarks in GAAP for direct and indirect costs. GAAP provides assurance that policies and procedures are applied uniformly.

Next, an allowable cost needs to be adequately documented. As in all sponsored agreements the role of documentation is critical to both reimbursable charges and conformity with any potential follow-on audit, whether that audit be performance or financially based.

Finally, allowable costs may not be included as a cost or used to meet cost sharing or matching requirements of any other federally financed program. The cost sharing of allocable costs must not be used from a prior period. In essence, the cost for the program must be incurred only for the program and in the period of the agreement.

Administrative, Direct, and Indirect Costs

In federally sponsored agreements there are three major categories of costs. Each organizational type, colleges and universities, nonprofit organizations, and state, local, and federally recognized Indian tribal governments, may have different terminology for allowable costs within these major cost categories. The terminology is important within each grantee's accounting system; however, the major cost categories are persistent throughout all organizational types. We begin by looking at the composition of the costs and documentation standards, which is followed by a discussion of each of the major categories of costs.

Composition of Cost

In federally sponsored agreements the composition of costs are important guidelines and principles. Let us look at the principle of total cost. The total cost of federally sponsored agreement is composed of the allowable direct cost of the program/research undertaking plus the allocable portion of allowable indirect costs less applicable credits. Applicable credits denote those receipts or reductions of expenditures (expenses) that operate to offset or reduce expense items. The most common examples of applicable credits include discounts and rebates on purchased items. Although discounts and rebates are obvious reductions in expenses, it is imperative that the grantee reduce expense items by these credits.

There is no universal rule for classifying costs as either direct or indirect for every accounting system. In fact, a cost may be direct to some specific service or function but indirect to the federally sponsored agreement or cost objective. This leads to a fair amount of discretion based on the cost objective and the specific accounting system. This means it is essential that each item of cost be treated consistently in like circumstances either as a direct or an indirect cost. This treatment is designed to assist the grantee in CAPN compliance and to provide assurance that the federal government will bear its fair share of total costs.

Documentation Standards

To provide clarity regarding the major categories of costs, four standards are articulated within the OMB Circulars. The first is that the grantee is responsible for ensuring that costs charged to a sponsored agreement are allowable, allocable, and reasonable. This standard identifies the responsibility for the financial charges for the sponsored agreement. Next, the grantee's financial management system is identified as an assurance process. The grantee's financial management system is to assure that no one person is to have complete control over all aspects of a financial transaction. This expectation of the financial management system is to assure segregation of duties and control within the grantee's systems. In addition, direct cost allocation principles are another aspect of documentation. When a cost is identified as benefiting two or more projects/activities and the proportions associated with the cost can be determined without undue effort or cost, a proportional allocation of the cost can be applied. Lastly, when a grantee authorizes the principal investigator (PI) or other individual to have primary responsibility for the management of sponsored agreement funds, the PI or designee's signature, initials, or use of a password is considered sufficient to meet the documentation requirements.

These identified standards allow the sponsor agreement to meet the CAPN. In the next section we demonstrate definitions of administrative, direct, and indirect costs as presented in the OMB Circulars and the CAPN.

Administrative Costs

An important aspect of administrative costs is that these costs can be considered as either direct or indirect costs. In many sponsored agreements, administrative costs are treated as indirect costs associated with overhead. However, this may not always be the case. An important guideline in the determination of the administrative costs as direct or indirect is to ensure that costs incurred for the same purpose in like circumstances are treated consistently as either direct or indirect costs. In certain circumstances direct charging of the salaries of administrative and clerical staff may be appropriate where a project requires an extensive amount of administrative or clerical support and the individuals involved can be specifically identified with the sponsored project. Direct charging of administrative and clerical staff requires documentation that the administrative and clerical staff used in the sponsored agreement is significantly greater than the routine level of administrative and clerical staff services.

There are multiple foundations for the allocation of administrative costs as indirect costs. The most common is found in universities and colleges where a rate is established between the grantor and grantee. This is most commonly identified on a modified total costs basis. The most prevalent example is when the costs of a student research assistant tuition are exempted from the total costs before applying the indirect rate. The rate and total cost basis are a function of the negotiations, which vary by organizational type and can be specific to a sponsored agreement. If an organization elects to accept a threshold rate, it is not required to perform a detailed analysis of its administrative costs, thereby reducing its financial accountability burden.

There are special issues for administrative costs associated with most state, local, and federally recognized Indian tribal governments. Given that many state, local, and federally recognized Indian tribal governments provide certain services, such as computer centers, purchasing, accounting, and so on, to operating agencies on a centralized basis, an allocation process for central service costs must be identified to allow assignment of benefited activities on a reasonable and consistent basis. Guidelines and illustrations of central service cost allocation plans are provided by the United States Department of Health and Human Services (1997).

Direct Costs

The definition of direct costs is focused on the cost objective. Direct costs are costs that can be identified specifically with a particular sponsored agreement or that can be directly assigned to the sponsored agreement with a high degree of accuracy and with minimal effort. As found with administrative costs, if a particular type of cost is treated as a direct cost for sponsored agreements, all costs incurred for the same purpose in similar circumstances shall be treated as direct costs. Typical direct costs chargeable to sponsored agreements include the compensation of employees specific to the performance of the agreement, costs associated with materials acquired, consumed, or expended specifically for the agreement, equipment and other approved capital expenditures associated with the agreement, and travel expenses incurred specifically to carry out the award. We specify some important aspects of one of the most important and critical direct costs, that of capital.

Capital

Although grantees are compensated for the use of their buildings, capital improvements, and equipment provided that they are used and properly allocable to sponsored agreements, the compensation is based on two allowable approaches, depreciation or use allowance. Purchased capital to fulfill the grantee's stated obligation in the sponsored agreement is treated independently from owned capital under CAPN.

One of the most identified difficulties found in the CAPN is the role of capital purchases. These purchases, whether they are for capital facilities or equipment, bring with them important limitations that require substantial consideration by the grantee. Guidelines are specific to each purchase and the amounts of those purchases. The Uniform Guidance reiterates these guidelines for grantees. Here we will note two important guidelines, those of equipment and those of capital improvements to land, building, or equipment. Both of these guidelines are specific within the CAPN and therefore need to be articulated.

The term *equipment* has a very specific meaning in the CAPN. Equipment is an article of nonexpendable, tangible personal property having a useful life of more than 1 year. In addition, equipment is an item having an acquisition cost, which equals or exceeds the lesser of the capitalization level established by the grantee for financial statement reporting purposes, or $5,000. Acquisition cost for equipment is the net purchase price of the equipment including the cost of any modifications required or desired to make it usable for its acquired purpose. If the grantee's regular accounting practice includes adding ancillary charges to the purchase price of the equipment, such as taxes, duty, transit insurance, freight, and installation, these ancillary charges must be included in the net purchase price of the equipment associated with the sponsored agreement.

There are two types of equipment, general purpose and special purpose. These definitions will directly impact the cost allowability of these equipment types. General purpose equipment is equipment that is not limited to research, medical, scientific or other technical activities. General purpose equipment can include office equipment and furnishings, information technology equipment and systems, reproduction and printing equipment, and motor vehicles. Special purpose equipment is equipment that is used for research, medical, scientific, or other technical activities only. Special purpose equipment can include microscopes, X-ray machines, and surgical instruments.

Why are equipment definitions and thresholds so important? Capital expenditures for general purpose equipment are unallowable as direct charges. The only exception to this rule for general purpose equipment is if the equipment was approved in advance by the awarding agency. Capital expenditures for special purpose equipment are allowable as direct costs, provided that items with a unit cost of $5,000 or more have the prior approval of the awarding agency.

What about capital improvements? Capital expenditures for improvements to land, buildings, or equipment that materially increase the value or useful life of the capital are unallowable as a direct cost except with the prior approval of the awarding agency.

These thresholds and definitions may have important impacts on grantees. Capital improvements are not directly chargeable, which means that they will need to be addressed through either a depreciation schedule based on useful life or, if a schedule is not available, then a use allowance may be put in place.

Indirect Costs

There are various methods used to allocate indirect costs based on the OMB Circular that is applied to the grantee. In general, indirect costs are those (a) incurred for a common or joint purpose benefiting more than one cost objective and (b) not readily assignable to the cost objectives specifically benefited, without effort disproportionate to the results achieved. The term *indirect costs* applies to costs originating with the grantee as well as costs incurred by others in supplying goods, services, and facilities. CAPN and the Uniform Guidance remind grantees that the allocations of indirect costs are focused on equitable, reasonable, and consistent processes used by the grantee. To facilitate equitable distribution of indirect expenses to the cost objectives served, it may be necessary to establish a number of pools of indirect costs. Indirect cost pools should be distributed to benefitted cost objectives on a basis that will produce an equitable result in consideration of relative benefits derived. Many indirect cost rates are negotiated with the granting agency or based on agreements with the federal government.

Applying CAPN to the Organization

The application of CAPN is an important and complex undertaking. We offer simple examples with the realization that more complex examples are prevalent for all grantees. We touched on some of this complexity when we defined equipment earlier in the chapter.

Example 1

As a new grantee university, you apply for a grant that incorporates a proposal for a disproportionate amount of administration to be performed. This is due to the fact that the federally sponsored agreement is for the purchase of important special equipment that has complex rules and regulations associated with the purchase. Normally, the university purchasing activity allocates its costs indirectly. These "normal" purchasing activity costs are allocated to both instruction and research on the basis of modified total costs. The university prefers to continue this allocation process. You build into your sponsored agreement these purchase costs and receive approval by the awarding agency. You directly charge theses costs to the sponsored agreement. Is this correct?

Yes. Given that these purchases are for special purpose equipment and approval has been obtained, these are direct costs to the sponsored agreement.

Example 2

As a nonprofit organization, you apply for a federally sponsored grant. Executive director Jones notes that included in the research grant is support for a half-time secretary, two laptops, and a smartphone. Are these types of costs appropriate?

Maybe. Administrative or clerical staff salaries are normally treated as indirect costs. These costs may be appropriate where a major project or activity explicitly budgets for administrative or clerical services and individuals involved can be specifically identified with the project or activity. Importantly, clarity must be shown in the accounting system, identifying the secretary with the sponsored agreement. CAPN considers the justification of general-use business items (e.g., laptop or smartphone) to determine if they are needed for a special research purpose. General office use is not sufficient justification, and the direct costs will be unallowable. Only materials and supplies actually used for the performance of a sponsored agreement may be charged as direct costs.

Example 3

Dr. Flower purchases a much-needed piece of specialized, scientific equipment for research on water penetration of concrete for a local bridge in XYZ city. When preparing the purchase request, Dr. Flower realizes that the only account with enough money to cover the costs of the scientific equipment is her other grant for research on water penetration of asphaltic cement. Because both grants are funded by the United States Department of Transportation, she charges the equipment to the asphaltic cement grant. Is this appropriate?

No. The cost principles in the OMB circulars and CAPN address four tests to determine the allowability of costs. The first is allocability. A cost is allocable to a specific grant if it is incurred solely to advance work under the grant and is deemed assignable, at least in part, to the grant. The second is reasonableness. A cost may be considered reasonable if the nature of the goods or services acquired reflect the action that a prudent person would have taken under the circumstances prevailing at the time of the decision to incur the cost. The third is consistency. Grantees must be consistent in assigning costs. Although costs may be charged as either direct or indirect costs, depending on their identifiable benefit to a particular sponsored agreement, they must be treated consistently for all work of the organization under similar circumstances, regardless of the source of funding. The final test is conformance. Conformance with the limitations and exclusions, as contained in the terms and conditions of the sponsored agreement, vary by type of activity, type of recipient, and other variables of individual awards.

Example 4

You receive an invoice from a PI in the office of sponsored programs at your university. The office supply store invoice identifies several items that are itemized as pens, envelopes, and paper clips. A second invoice from Red's Donuts is included. A note from the PI states the following: The office supplies were need to replenish my supplies that were used on this sponsored agreement. The donuts were used in our weekly staff meeting that discussed our progress on the sponsored agreement. Do you accept these invoices and charge them to the sponsored agreement?

No. If the office supplies are not specifically allocable to the grant, they are considered general office supplies and should not be charged as a direct cost to the grant account. Entertainment costs, such as food, are unallowable. Meals are allowable on a research grant when they are provided to subjects or patients under study provided that such charges are not duplicated in participant's per diem or subsistence allowances and such costs are specifically approved as part of the project activity.

Meals may be an allowable cost, on a research grant, if they are provided in conjunction with a meeting when the primary purpose is to disseminate technical information. An institution must also have a written and enforceable policy in place that (1) ensures consistent charging of meal costs, (2) defines what constitutes a meeting for the dissemination of technical information, (3) specifies when meals are allowable for such meetings, and (4) establishes limitations and other controls on this cost. Recurring business meetings, such as staff meetings, are generally not considered meetings to disseminate technical information.

What Is IAS 20?

This chapter has previously discussed the cost accounting norms (CAPN) that are utilized in the accounting of governmental grants in the United States. The authority of the CAPN, however, is limited in that it is applicable only to organizations based in the United States. Not all governmental grants, however, are constrained within the borders of the United States. From time to time some grants issued by governments in the United States are awarded to organizations located abroad. Similarly, many organizations based in the United States receive grants from foreign governments. In the first case, foreign organizations are not set up to meet the accounting practices established by the Financial Accounting Foundation (FAF) and are thus ill-equipped to adhere to CAPN. In the second case, United States–based organizations operating overseas may be subject to FAF guidelines, but the accounting rule requirements of the granting governments will differ.

Directing the accounting practices on the international landscape is the International Accounting Standards Committee (IASC). Established in

1973, and restructured as the International Accounting Standards Board in 2001, the IASC was tasked with the creation of principles-based accounting standards for use on a global scale (Camfferman & Zeff, 2007). While a rules-based approach, such as the system of accounting utilized in the United States, is focused on the objective of comparability and verifiability, a principle-based approach to accounting is centered on the objective of providing guidance that leads to good financial reporting (Benston, Bromwich, & Wagenhofer, 2006). The result of the committee's work is a series of principles referred to as the International Accounting Standards (IAS) that are used in more than 115 countries and to which adherence is required for listing on most foreign exchanges (Kieso, Weygandt, & Warfield, 2011).

Given the prevalence of government-funded programs around the world, a key issue for the IASC early on was the creation of a standard that addressed government grants and other forms of assistance. After all, the receipt of government assistance could be important to the accurate reporting of an organization's financial statements, and such an importance would require that an appropriate method of accounting be followed. The development of this method came in 1982 with the creation of IAS 20 (Camfferman & Zeff, 2007).

Titled as *Accounting for Government Grants and Disclosure of Government Assistance*, IAS 20 addresses issues related to the treatment and disclosure of a governmental grant and the disclosure requirements for governmental assistance (Epstein & Mirza, 2000). Although a grant is technically a form of government assistance, IAS 20 provides a distinction between grants and other forms of assistance due to the differences of how they are treated in the accounting process and their requirements for disclosure in the financial reports. According to the standard, assistance refers to an action by a government with the intent to provide an economic benefit to a specific organization or range of organizations under an established criterion (International Financial Reporting Standards Foundation, 2012). A grant, on the other hand, is assistance from a government in the form of a transfer of resources in exchange for complying with a set of conditions related to the operation of the receiving organization. The transfer of resources for a grant can be either monetary or nonmonetary (Epstein & Mirza, 2000).

Within IAS 20 there are two types of grants: those related to assets and those related to income. Grants whose primary condition include the acquisition of long-term assets are referred to as "grants related to assets." Alternatively, all grants other than those related to assets are referred to as "grants related to income." In both cases the grant should be recognized as income on a systematic basis over the periods in which the organization recognizes expenses for the related costs that are intended by the grant. In the case of grants related to income, this recognition takes place when costs are incurred, allowing a direct association between the resources received from the grant and the meeting of operational activities as established in the grant's conditions. For grants related to assets, the recognition of income is

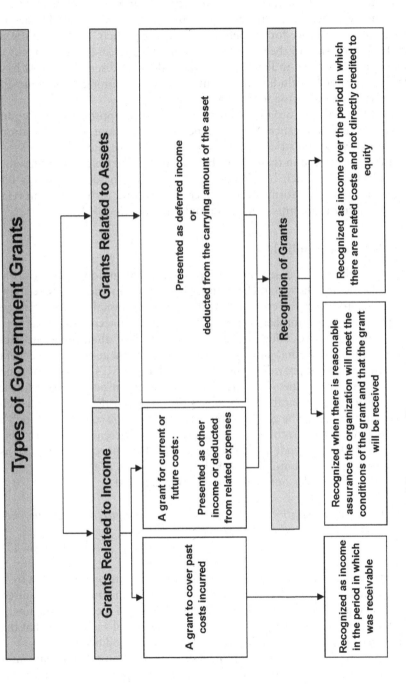

Figure 5.1 IAS 20's Treatment of Government Grants

either deferred until the operational activities associated with the grant are complete or they are deducted from the carrying amount of the asset. While the standard provides two means of accounting for grants related to assets, it lays out a preference for the deferred income approach (Epstein & Mirza, 2000). An overview of the types of government grants and their recognition as income is provided in Figure 5.1. A more detailed discussion about how IAS 20 is applied, including its use in the cost accounting of government grants, is discussed in the following section.

IAS 20 provides a broad perspective on how to appropriately account for government assistance on the financial statements of an organization, but it has two key restrictions in its use. First, it does not apply to assistance that is received in the form of benefits in the determination of taxable income. However, such benefits are not typically provided by grants but rather through other forms of assistance. The second restriction is in relation to agricultural grants, which fall under the purview of IAS 41.

How Is IAS 20 Applied?

IAS 20 is primarily focused on the appropriate recognition of government grants as income; however, the standard directly ties the grants recognition as income with the cost of providing an operational activity. This tie provides the connection between IAS 20 and the cost accounting of grants, but it does so by providing guidance on how to best align the grant with incurred costs rather than how to measure the costs themselves. The benefit of this approach is it provides a means by which the IASC's objective of good financial reporting is met while also allowing the organization to pursue the consistency and comparability objectives of the more rules-based approach for cost accounting. The guidance for this connection is achieved through a series of rules for the recognition of grants under different conditions. This section intends to provide an understanding of the connection of IAS 20 as it applies to cost accounting by providing an overview of these rules.

The first of the rules outlined by the standard is that

> [g]rants in recognition of specific costs are recognized as income over the same period as the relevant expense.
>
> (IAS 20, para. 17)

The intent of this rule is to defer recognition of any income provided by a grant until such a time that the grant is expended in pursuit of its required operational activity. This allows for the recognition of income in the financial statements as it is earned by the organization. Until such a time that the grant is earned, it may be subject to cancellation or modification.

The process for the recognition must also be done on a "systematic and rational basis." This is best illustrated with an example. Suppose an organization receives a $9 million grant for housing services to homeless veterans for a 3-year period. Costs for the services equal $6 million and are incurred as follows in Table 5.1.

As the rule states that the grant must be recognized as income over the period that matches the costs incurred using a systematic process, the total grant would be recognized as follows in Table 5.2.

The second rule states that

> [g]rants related to depreciable assets are usually recognized as income over the periods and in the proportions in which depreciation on those assets is charge.

(IAS 20, para. 17)

Here, income from a grant is to be deferred by spreading the income across the life of the depreciable asset. Using the same organization from the previous example, suppose they received a second grant in the amount of $10 million to construct a homeless shelter. The organization, however, estimated the cost of the shelter at $20 million. If the shelter is depreciated using the straight-line method of a period of 10 years, then $1 million of the grant would be recognized as income in each of the 10 years.

The application of IAS 20 can be further witnessed in the third rule, which explains that

> [g]rants related to nondepreciable assets may also require the fulfillment of certain obligations and would then be recognized as income over periods which bear the cost of meeting the obligation.

(IAS 20, para. 20)

Not all costs incurred involve depreciable assets. Some organizations may even receive grants to cover the purchase of assets such as land. Grants

Table 5.1 Grant Illustration 1

Year	Costs
1	$1 million
2	$2 million
3	$3 million

Table 5.2 Grant Illustration 2

Year	Grant Recognized
1	$9 × (1/6) = $1.5 million
2	$9 × (2/6) = $3 million
3	$9 × (3/6) = $4.5 million

issued by governments in the United States typically place limitations on the use of grants to purchase land, but it is more common in third-world countries, where the government is reliant on nonprofit organizations to provide key services and the gift of land is seen as improving the operational means of the organization. When a grant involves such nondepreciable assets, the income received from the grant is not able to be spread over the useful life of an asset as no measurable life exists. This is accommodated for in the standard by spreading the income received from the grant over the duration of the obligated activity and at fair value.

An example of this rule can be seen from the perspective of an organization receiving a grant of land. The grant, however, was conditioned that a facility be built upon the land, the construction of which is expected to take 3 years and is estimated to cost $40 million. In each of the first 2 years of the project, $10 million is spent on construction, followed by $20 million in the third year. The fair value of the land is estimated at $50 million. In accordance with the rule, the organization would need to recognize the fair value of the grant over the 3-year construction period. Accordingly, the grant would be recognized as shown in Table 5.3.

Next, the fourth rule created by IAS 20 explains that

> [g]rants are sometimes received as part of a package of financial or fiscal aids to which a number of conditions are attached.
>
> (IAS 20, para. 19)

A grant can be issued with different conditions attached to different aspects of the operational activity. When this occurs, the terms of the grant must be evaluated to determine the proper apportionment of the revenue to each of the conditions. If, for example, a grant was issued to a nonprofit for the construction of a veterans housing facility and for subsidizing the cost of providing job training to the residents of the facility, the grant would be apportioned as a grant related to assets or grant related to income based on the portion of the grant that is dedicated to the construction. The portion related to the construction would be recognized over the useful life of the facility, as outlined in the second rule. The remaining portion of the grant would be recognized across the period in which costs associated with the job training are expended, as outlined in the first rule.

Table 5.3 Grant Illustration 3

Year	Grant Recognized
1	$50 × (1/4) = $12.5 million
2	$50 × (1/4) = $12.5 million
3	$50 × (2/4) = $25 million

The fifth and final rule states that

> *[a] government grant that becomes receivable as compensation for expenses or losses already incurred or for the purpose of giving immediate financial support to the enterprise with no future related costs should be recognized as income of the period in which it becomes receivable, as an extraordinary item if appropriate.*
>
> (IAS 20, para. 20)

Occasionally, grants have been awarded by governments with the intent of providing immediate financial support to an organization. These grants are awarded with the specific intent to compensate for past losses that the organization has incurred. Such losses may have been incurred by an organization that was providing assistance in the aftermath of a natural disaster or by an organization facing financial insolvency. Regardless of the reason that a grant may be needed, the intent is to encourage a certain set of behaviors. In the case of an organization assisting after a natural disaster, the grant would encourage future involvement by nonprofits by compensating for lost resources. In the case of the insolvent organization, the grant would provide the capacity for an organization whose existence is viewed as positive or essential to carry on. Grants of this nature should be recognized as income in the year in which it was received.

Conclusion

This chapter has sought to identify and discuss the principles and norms for determining costs applicable to grants, contracts, and other agreements with the federal government. Particular attention was paid to how the principles and norms influence the grantsmanship of educational institutions, nonprofit organizations, and state, local and Indian tribal governments. The intent of the principles and norms is not to control the costs associated with the grants issued by the federal government, but rather to establish a uniform approach of costing and to promote effective program delivery and efficiency.

The successful application of cost accounting principles requires development of a mutual understanding between representatives of grantee institutions and the federal government as to their scope, implementation, and interpretation of costs. In the United States, this is accomplished with the publication of the federal governments cost accounting norms and principles as they relate to educational, nonprofit, and state, local, and Indian tribal governments in OMB Circulars A-21, A-122, and A-87. These standards are centered on a rules-based approach to accounting that establishes the allowability of a cost to be counted against a grant. For organizations that are dealing with grants on an international level, IAS 20 also directs costing behavior. As a principles-based approach, the intent of the standard is to help grantees produce appropriate financial reporting. The discussion of these standards, however, is by no means all inclusive. As circumstances change, the timing and definitions they utilize may also be adjusted. As such, readers are encouraged to review the Uniform Guidance, as provided by the Federal Register.

Notes

1 Federal and nonfederal organizations are construed to include cabinets, agencies, departments, and other federal and nonfederal organizations.
2 Although many would consider local governments as instrumentalities or agencies of a state, local governments are defined independently of the state for this OMB Circular regardless of powers afforded to the local government by the state.
3 This definition includes any native village as defined in Section 3 of the Alaska Native Claims Settlement Act, 85 Stat. 688.

References

Benston, G. J., Bromwich, M., & Wagenhofer, A. (2006). Principles- versus rules-based accounting standards: The FASB's standard setting strategy. *ABACUS*, 42(2), 165–188.

Camfferman, K., & Zeff, S. A. (2007). *Financial reporting and global capital markets: A history of the international accounting standards committee, 1973–2000.* New York: Oxford University Press.

Epstein, B. J., & Mirza, A. A. (2000). *WILEY IAS 2000: Interpretation and application of international accounting standards 2000.* Somerset, NJ: John Wiley and Sons.

International Financial Reporting Standards Foundation. (2012). *Technical summary: IAS 20 accounting for government grants and disclosure of government assistance.* Retrieved from http://www.ifrs.org/documents/ias20.pdf

Kieso, D. E., Weygandt, J. J., & Warfield, T. D. (2011). *Intermediate accounting (IFRS ed.).* Hoboken, NJ: John Wiley and Sons.

Mader, D. (2014). *M-14–17: Metrics for uniform guidance (2 C.F.R. 200)* [Memorandum]. Washington, DC: Office of Management and Budget.

Office of Management and Budget. (2004a). *OMB circular A-21: Cost principles for educational institutions.* Retrieved from https://www.whitehouse.gov/omb/circulars_a021_2004/

Office of Management and Budget. (2004b). *OMB circular A-122: Cost principles for non-profit organizations.* Retrieved from https://www.whitehouse.gov/omb/circulars_a122_2004/

Office of Management and Budget. (2004c). *OMB circular A-87: Cost principles for state, local, and Indian tribal governments.* Retrieved from https://www.whitehouse.gov/omb/circulars_a087_2004/

Office of Management and Budget. (2013). *Uniform administrative requirements, cost principles, and audit requirements for federal awards—final guidance.* Retrieved from https://federalregister.gov/a/2013–30465

Uniform administrative requirements, cost principles, and audit requirements for federal awards, 2 CFR 200 (2013).

United States Department of Health and Human Services. (1997). *A guide for state and local government agencies: Cost principles and procedures for establishing cost allocation plans and indirect cost rates for grants and contracts with the federal government.* Retrieved from http://www.dol.gov/oasam/boc/asmb_c-10.pdf

6 Cost Management Innovations in Federal Agencies

Dale R. Geiger

Budget control and clean external audit opinions are the primary aspirations of most federal accounting organizations. Good financial management is considered to be "spending 99.9% of the budget appropriation." Severe penalties for overspending the budget exist, and underspending is considered a disservice to the organization as it is evidence that future budgets can be cut. Of course, simply spending the 99.9% of the budget ignores the question of how well the budget is spent in support of missions. Some federal organizations are using cost accounting to develop actionable, internal views of resource consumption in efforts to boost mission effectiveness.

Cost accounting data feed external and internal needs. In federal agencies, external needs are mandated by laws, higher headquarters, or regulatory oversight agencies, and organizations develop cost accounting to comply with reporting requirements. Leaders can create internal information requirements to accomplish or enhance their organization's mission as they seek to create a continuously more cost-effective organization.

It is budget reductions and fiscal constraints that often stimulate leaders of government operations to act. The first response often sees elaborate efforts to "market" the resource needs of the organization to the budget-granting power. If this effort fails, severe budget shortfalls then result in cutbacks to the organization's mission. Services are cut, service levels degraded, or in the case of the Department of Defense national security assets are eliminated.

Neither of these two responses stimulates any learning or creativity into how the organization might use resources more cost-effectively. Furthermore, the subset of missions left after downsizing is under no pressure to change. For them, it is simply business as usual. Since there is no apparent stimulation for continuous improvement, the net result is often a continuous decline in efficiency, mission effectiveness, and mission breadth.

However, some leaders are challenging these common responses by innovating a third alternative: a management approach that institutionalizes cost management and control. These leaders recognize that the management of operations becomes increasingly important in accomplishing the missions of government as the fiscal resources of government become increasingly constrained.

These leaders demonstrate sustained capabilities in continuous improvement in one or both of two ways. One formalizes cost–benefit analysis for large, nonrecurring decisions and the other builds cost management and control processes to drive ongoing operations. While cost management and control processes appear to be customized to the organization, its mission, and its environment, several different forms of cost-managed organizations have been identified: organization based, role based, and output based, and all exhibit a number of similar attributes that can be thought of as requirements for success (Geiger, 2011). The purpose of this chapter is to consider and contrast the cost accounting requirements of these successful innovations, which is in contrast to some reports that cost accounting and continuous improvement are failing in federal government agencies (Martin, 2005, 2007).

The "Good Idea Fairy" Ignores Cost

The "good idea fairy" is the Pentagon label for suggestions that often appear late during decision-making processes. While constructive suggestions are a very good thing, the term has come to have a disruptive connotation. The problem stems from that fact that good ideas always show benefits but seldom consider costs. Any benefit appears attractive when cost is zero or ignored.

Consider the experience of a cost-conscious staff officer assigned to the army's G1 office. G1, as the army's personnel department, is responsible for funding military payroll and many other areas involving soldier welfare and support. His story, which follows, relates to experiences as an advisor to the G1's representative to the Army Uniform Board (AUB) that meets annually to recommend changes to army-provided soldier uniforms and gear. The voting members of the AUB are primarily senior officers and executives representing various commands and areas:

> *The process would go something like this: The Army would table a requirement or suggestion for improving Army clothing/uniforms and then contractors and vendors would pitch the Army on "new and improved" clothing items. My first AUB experience felt like I was at a runway fashion show; the vendors had models and samples of new fitness uniforms, new softer and more absorbent towels, new socks, and of course new Army battle dress uniforms, as well as several recommendations for improvements to current uniforms.*
>
> *I watched in amazement as a new item was shown to the board, and then everyone was asked to vote on the item to determine if the Army should purchase and field it. The vote went around the table and, for each item, everyone voted yes. If cost was mentioned it would be a simple statement of initial costs or a slight increase in cost per item.*

Following the board the Army Chief of Staff would approve the results and then it became a mandatory requirement to fund. When I had to fund all the new items I was amazed at how much the bill became for the Army. Some items that only add a few dollars of expense became millions of dollars in FYDP[1] costs due to the volume the Army purchases to change out and sustain the Army. As an example, with 80,000 new recruits each year, an improved towel that costs $1.00 more, is $80,000 extra per year or $400,000 over the FYDP plus the sustainment costs which the Army pays every enlisted soldier a clothing allowance each year. That year the budget went up by $40 million dollars (for one year!).

My second AUB was similar. However, I recommended non-concur to every item that increased costs to the Army. But everything was still approved as only the G1, G8 and Army Budget Office non-concurred to new items due to increased costs.

My third AUB I worked with the Army G4 staff and was able to provide costing data to each item for initial purchase costs, buy out, incremental, and FY costs; and then totaled over the FYDP. With the costs front and center, the votes drastically changed to non-concur for all new items. In addition, we imposed additional requirements on any new items to determine offsets. Cost identification and requests for offsets greatly reduced the appetite for new items and minimized changes to current clothing items.

The following year some items were approved, however, the leadership had to take a hard look at the costs and find offsets (mostly by reducing other item costs). The AUB started looking at all the clothing bag items and trying to find cost savings in order to pay for new requirements and better equipment.

Bottom line: Providing cost data changed the behavior of the AUB to become more cost aware and efficient.[2]

The Army's Eight-Step Cost–Benefit Analysis Process

In 2009 Mr. Steve Bagby, deputy assistant secretary of the army for cost and economics, was tasked to develop a formal process to consider both cost and benefits of major proposals. His efforts led to the Eight-Step Cost–Benefit Analysis process that became a requirement for all large projects submitted to the Pentagon. The tasking came from the highest levels of the army as the "good idea fairy" was hard at work in even the most senior ranks.

Subordinates, often at very high rank themselves, would bring new ideas to their attention, and those ideas usually had compelling and desirable benefits. Cost, on the other hand, was not included in the brief, and this omission made it very difficult, if not impossible, for senior leaders to rationally balance trade-offs with existing budget requirements and competing ideas.

Often this exercise was thought to be a frustrating waste of time. Consider the following vignette from a subsequent army training session course explaining the origin of the cost–benefit analysis (CBA) process:

> *Too often we were treating cost as an afterthought at the headquarters: which is why the Chief of Staff, General Casey[3] himself, really wanted this. Why? What was happening? He would take a brief by a Command somewhere with a great idea to do something operationally that was very important in their estimation. So he would take the brief and the briefer would say something like, "Sir, this is of utmost importance and here are the strategic reasons we should do this and here are the operational capabilities it will give us. This is how we think we can win the war."*
>
> *Pretty strong briefings. He would get all kinds of these, every day. Then the briefer would say, "Subject to any more questions, thank you Sir, we really hope you think this was a good idea." And he would say "Yes, I think this is a great idea." And they would walk away and General Casey would turn to General Stanton and General Marcs, people on the funding side, and he would say "So how are we going to do this?" And they would say, "Sir we have no idea." Funding was treated as an afterthought because from the briefer's perspective the output was most important whether it was a warfighting capability or whether it was to get greater operational capacity. The funding was not an issue. So what we are trying to do is consider cost up front.[4]*

Development of the CBA process was challenging. CBA models steeped in economic theory can go to great lengths in trying to calculate benefits and even externalities. On the other hand, some cost accounting texts hardly mention the subject. The basic idea of CBA, that both costs and benefits must be considered, is very simple. That concept implicitly drives all decision making that is not emotional, habitual, or reflexive.

The process of choosing from a dinner menu illustrates some of the issues in CBA. Nobody chooses randomly or automatically takes the least costly option. We go through a decision process. It starts with an objective: We are hungry and want to eat. We have some baseline facts: things like spending limits, location, time available for eating, calorie goals, and tastes. The menu gives us alternatives, and the cost is conveniently stated. We consider the relative benefits and appeal of each menu item and weigh the alternatives on the basis of some, often unstated and subjective, selection criteria. We make a decision and live with it.

The army's Eight-Step Cost–Benefit Analysis process mirrors the dinner menu choice example: resulting in a very practical approach that accepts a level of subjectivity while seeking cost-informed, not cost-dominated, decisions. Furthermore, the process injects consistency and rigor to the costing while seeking to encourage learning rather than mere compliance.

Rigor and consistency in the costing effort are ensured by requiring that all CBAs submitted to army headquarters are reviewed by the Office of the Deputy Assistant Secretary of the Army for Cost and Economics. The review process does not comment on alternative or decision criteria selection assumptions. It does not critique subjective assumptions on relative benefits. It concentrates on verifying that the cost data is complete, accurate, and adequately sourced.

The *first step* requires the proposal to **Define the Problem or Opportunity**. The intent here is a clear and unambiguous statement that of what the proposal is seeking to fix or improve for the entire army enterprise. The enterprise aspect ensures that the proposal does not benefit one part of the organization at the expense of another.

The *second step* requires the proposal to **Define the Scope; Formulate Facts and Assumptions**. A clear statement of assumptions is important for the reviewer to understand the logic and thought process in the proposal. Assumptions are inherently subjective and can be judged by the reviewer. Facts are empirically true and can be supported by evidence. With sufficient time and resources, some assumptions can be converted to facts.

The *third step* asks the proposer to **Define the Alternatives**. Alternatives are the potential solutions to the problem statement. The status quo, no action, is required as one alternative, and army guidance seeks to have several other potential courses of action under consideration. The goal here is to encourage creative thinking and avoid the common problem of the proposer having a predetermined outcome with the CBA proposal being a marketing platform.

The *fourth step* requires the proposal to **Develop Cost Estimates for Each Alternative**. The requirement here is for the total cost of each alternative over its life cycle. These include onetime and recurring costs. Each alternative course of action must use the same assumptions and facts previously stated in step two to ensure valid comparison of alternatives. Costs are required to be documented from valid, official sources.

The *fifth step* asks the proposer to **Identify Quantifiable and Nonquantifiable Benefits**. Quantifiable benefits are measurable and can be supported by evidence and facts. Nonquantifiable benefits generally cannot be measured at all, or not with reasonable accuracy, and are often based on the opinions of subject matter experts. This step recognizes the inherent subjectivity inherent in the process and simply seeks to make those judgments clear.

The *sixth step* directs the proposer to **Define Alternative Selection Criteria**. This step seeks to understand how the proposer intends to weigh the various elements of costs and benefits in coming to a decision. A clear statement of criteria allows the reviewer to assess if they have been unrealistically skewed to favor one alternative or disqualify another.

The *seventh step* seeks a **Comparison of Alternatives**. This step results in one of the alternatives showing superiority. The intent is to foster thought as to the robustness of that superiority, possible second- and third-order effects, and sensitivity to changes in assumptions or conditions.

The *eighth step* specifies that the proposal *Report Results and Recommendations*. This step asks for a narrative and decision briefing that summarizes the analysis and makes concluding statements about the comparison of alternatives. It should end with a firm recommendation for the preferred alternative.

The results of the Eight-Step Cost–Benefit Analysis process have exceeded expectations. Senior army leaders feel that the cost-effectiveness of major program and policy decision quality has improved significantly even though the low-cost alternative has been selected only about half of the time. The major benefit seems to be that learning occurs, and creativity is enabled when logically and carefully thinking through the eight steps.

Proposers report that the process is not linear: going through each of the steps in order. It is often the case that Step 4 (Cost Evaluation), Step 5 (Benefit Identification), or Step 6 (Selection Criteria Definition) result in the creation of a new, and often improved, alternative. The proposer then circles back to Step 3 (Alternative Definition) and continues from there. Learning also can result in changing Step 2 (Assumptions), which can also potentially change downstream steps.

The eight-step process requirement has also undoubtedly resulted in many proposals never reaching senior leaders as proposers recognized the infeasibility or unattractiveness of their ideas themselves. The process's requirement for enterprise-wide consideration of cost and benefit encourages this phenomenon.

The value of the Eight-Step Cost–Benefit Analysis process has also been recognized by at least some of the subordinate organizations bringing proposals to the Pentagon. Forces Command (FORSCOM), the largest command in the army, began its own internal CBA process in August 2013. They used the same eight-step process developed in the Pentagon to simplify implementation and training. FORSCOM policy began to require CBAs at the weekly meetings where the senior officers made decisions on large contracts, those over $300,000, and other strategic decisions such as moving units from one base to another.

The initial response of subordinates was resistance in many cases.[5] This ran the gamut from anger to avoidance. Senior officers, however, quickly realized the difference in decision briefings that were in CBA format and those that weren't. Subordinates quickly realized that requests without a CBA were less likely to be approved. By September, the command felt that it had a fully functioning CBA process as senior leaders affirmed their requirement for CBAs that "removed ambiguity" and allowed them to ask the right questions to "make it easier to make a good decision."

If institutionalization is not enough evidence of success, it seems clear that significant cost savings and cost avoidances have occurred. Although this may be difficult to quantify in some cases, the command feels that the

CBA program has yielded $507M since its start some 26 months ago with $263M occurring in the last 12 months.[6]

Furthermore, it was felt that the process allowed leaders to spend more time and effort on risk assessment and sensitivity analysis. Leaders felt their decisions were "more scientific" being based on facts rather than on narratives and opinions. Ken Graham, FORSCOM cost accounting manager, sums up the program and his staff's involvement:

> We review all CBAs before they go to the CARB (Contract and Acquisition Review Board) and then on to the senior staff. Sometimes we send them back for a redo when it's clear that they haven't burned enough brain cells. Our goal is to position ourselves as helping the requester get the right cost estimates and prepare for the obvious questions they will get.
>
> The results have exceeded our expectations. We are in a target-rich environment with Cost Benefit Analysis. It isn't just a matter of low hanging fruit: it's lying on the ground and we're helping to pick it up and apply it to the mission. We are getting the good decisions we want and believe that this has been done without risk to our readiness mission.

To enhance the credibility of the analyses, the Office of the Deputy Assistant Secretary of the Army for Cost and Economics maintains several highly detailed databases that can source the CBA process. One, AMCOS (the Army Military and Civilian Costing System), provides current cost data for numerous elements of military pay for each rank and military specialty. These elements include base pay, housing allowance, retirement benefit accrual, and GI education accrual, and AMCOS reports them by appropriation area. The second, the FORCES Model, provides similarly current and detailed cost data for all equipment, munitions, supplies, and consumables and offers options for building military organizations and or moving them from one location to another.

Not All Decisions Justify a Formal CBA: The Case for Cost Management and Control

The logic that costs and benefits must be weighed applies to cost–benefit analysis itself. Consider doing a cost–benefit analysis on the Eight-Step Cost–Benefit Analysis process. There are certainly costs of doing the formal report, evaluating the cost estimates, and documenting each step. That is not something that would be justified if there is only a small benefit involved as in the menu-choice decision mentioned earlier. The cost of the CBA process would exceed the benefit of the CBA process. Therefore, a rigorous CBA process makes the most sense for larger, and typically nonrecurring, decisions that justify the effort.

Some other process is needed to drive cost effectiveness into the multitude of day-to-day decisions that occur in large organizations. Complex, ongoing, and continuous operations need a cost management and control process in which leadership can institutionalize continuous process improvement. This implies a leadership-driven management process where creativity is enabled. Furthermore, such a process would avoid micromanagement or over regulation: Processes that stifle creativity and learning encourage only mindless compliance.

Military operations are a good model to consider the difference between the CBA process and the leadership driven management process. Considerable thought and analysis go into making the strategic decisions. This is inherently like a CBA process where military benefits are weighed versus military costs in personnel and capabilities. On the other hand, tactical operations conducted by small units and even individuals must occur rapidly, if not instantly. There is not time for detailed analysis and consideration of multiple courses of action. Likewise, it is not physically possible for the high command to make every decision.

Most battlefield decisions are decentralized and subordinates are given direction through general orders and guidance through "Statements of Commander's Intent." The organization trains subordinates extensively in understanding their jobs and emphasizes the need for continuous learning and improvement. The After-Action Review is the key step in the continuous improvement process. These reviews look at three questions: "What was expected?" "What actually happened?" and "Why was there a difference?" The goal of the review exercise is to learn from experience through constructive accountability and to stimulate the creativity of the team to improve performance is the future. The emphasis is on fixing problems rather than on fixing blame.

This military command and control template has proved valuable in cost management and control. Plans, budgets, forecasts, or even prior period performance can *create the expectation* for cost performance. Cost accounting tells *what actually happened*, and then the cost After-Action Review requires the subordinate team to explain *why actual cost varied from expectation*. The subordinate team must then also explain what is being done to fix problems and how they will improve performance in the future. Furthermore, since cost variances are quantified, big problems can be differentiated from small problems: further facilitating efficiency by enabling management by exception.

Organization-Based Cost Management and Control

Three distinctly different applications of this cost management and control template have been documented as successful (Geiger, 2000, 2010). Organization-Based Control is the simplest from a cost accounting perspective. This paradigm utilizes the organization chart with its inherent, preexisting accountability relationships and creates the cost After Action Review discussion at nodes on the organizational chart. The cost accounting requirements are very basic: a responsibility costing or cost center concept for each organization.

The army garrison at Fort Huachuca, Arizona, provided the initial site for this innovation in 1997 (Geiger, 2011). Garrisons run the operations of the military installation in much the same manner as a city or town. The internal review manager, James Freauff, was the change agent:

> *As budgets get cut year after year, it seems to me that there has to be a better way to use increasingly limited resources. There must be a systematic management process of continuous improvement that would be far better than mindlessly cutting x% of our capability every time there's an x% budget cut.*
>
> *(Geiger, 2011, p. 100)*

His supervisor, Garrison Commander Colonel Ted Chopin, was motivated by a desire to make a difference in the common scenario where subordinates view their budget allocations as entitlements with a mandate to spend:

> *When I took command it was clear that I had no real way of impacting much. All the budget was distributed to my subordinates and there was nothing left to play with. I needed a process that would free up resources for me to command if I was going to make a contribution personally.*
>
> *(Geiger, 2011, p. 104)*

After training on the successes and lessons learned at Fort Huachuca, the army garrison at Fort Belvoir, Virginia, began its Organization-Based Control process in 2015. In this case the resource manager,[7] Mike Bidelman, filled the change-agent role, and his supervisor, Steven Brooks, deputy garrison commander, led the effort. Brooks's vision for the cost management and control effort is to improve the mission effectiveness of the garrison in providing for the soldiers and tenant organization on Fort Belvoir:

> *The last ten years has seen our mission increase from serving 22,000 to 50,000 people on Fort Belvoir while our staff has declined. Finding efficiencies is now a necessity. Furthermore, I also believe that being a good steward of the taxpayer's money is a responsibility of leaders at all levels.*[8]

Bidelman summarizes the progress in the first months of operation:

> *Building the skillset of cost analysis tools gave us a rapid return on investment. For example, the Golf course saved over $300,000 in the*

*last year by rethinking their operations. This skillset has suffered greatly
as financial reporting and audit readiness have dominated the resource
management community lately.*[9]

Role-Based Cost Management and Control

The second documented successful paradigm is Role-Based Control. This
methodology creates accountability relationships where none currently
exist in the organization chart. For example, certain costs may be budgeted
or have reporting relationships at high levels of the organization. These
resources appear to be free to the consuming organization: never a good
environment where cost effectiveness is desired. This paradigm offers value
in the very frequent situation where support cost elements such as facilities, information systems, contracting are centralized. Responsibility costing
augmented by a causally based allocation process meets the cost accounting
requirements.

The Role-Based Control paradigm creates a cost After-Action Review,
where the support organizations explain their expected cost, actual cost,
and cost variances to the organizations they support. It also offers promise
where certain costs, military payroll for example, are not accounted for at
subordinate levels.

The Navy Research and Development Laboratory case study (Geiger,
2011) illustrated two major innovations. The first was the beneficial interac-
tion between support providers and consumers provided by the cost After-
Action Review. The budgeting process funded both the supported and the
supporting organizations independently. This means support costs are not
part of the supported organization's budget, and it appears quite common
that support is over consumed when it is "free" to the consumer. In Role-
Based Cost Management and Control the support provider briefs the support consumer in the cost After-Action Review. The fact that this monthly
meeting has continued for more than 15 years seems to indicate that both
parties value this dialog.

The second major innovation in this process stems from improving the
cost accounting allocation methodology. Previously support costs were
allocated on the basis of labor hours. This appears to be a very common
practice as labor is measured frequently and accurately. However, its relationship to support cost consumption is problematic except for, perhaps,
a human relations support function where labor hour distribution may be
roughly equivalent to support consumption.

Using labor hours to distribute facilities cost, for example, made little
sense. The Laboratory was occupying every square foot available even
though some of the space had been built as temporary during World War II.
When one department's work and workforce declined, its facilities allocation did too, even though it was occupying the same space. There was simply no incentive to free up any space for others to use. On the other hand,

another department that was growing rapidly could find no space for its new hires and its space per person was half that of the declining department at the time of the case study.

Changing the basis of allocation to square footage immediately changed behaviors of those who now saw the cost of their facility usage. This proved to be a major benefit as it generated many efficiencies and even allowed those temporary spaces to finally be torn down.

Output-Based Cost Management and Control

The third observed cost control paradigm focuses control on the organization's output of goods or services: an Output-Based Control process. Here, the cost accounting requirement is more complex as costs must be accumulated by each good or service provided by the organization. This often requires unique cost accounting attention. For example, the time and attendance system might require employees' input as to where their time was spent. Materials might also be tracked directly to their final use. Overhead and other indirect costs most likely require an allocation process to assign their cost to each output using cause-and-effect relationships as in the Role-Based example.

Many government organizations are not funded via appropriation and may be candidates for an Output-Based Control process: particularly when they seek cost-based justification for their price or user fee determinations. These are known by various names such as working capital fund, internal support fund, enterprise fund, and others. Geiger, 2011 documented the example of the Treasury Department's Bureau of Engraving and Printing (BEP).

As a working capital fund, BEP receives funds by charging its customers for its output. Currently, the vast majority of its sales come from the Federal Reserve System in payment for printing currency. Thirty years ago, the United States Post Office was also a large customer as the bureau printed all the nation's stamps.

It was, perhaps, the post office initiative to compete stamp printing that drove much of BEP's motivation to innovate its cost accounting and its cost management and control processes. The problem derived from the inadequacies of its costing methodology when it was asked to bid against private printers for individual stamp issues. Low-volume, highly complex, large, multi-image commemorative stamps cost considerably more per unit than do the high-volume, simple, small, single-image bulk stamps. While its cost accounting arguably provided accurate *total* cost it was apparently unable to distinguish the costs of various stamp jobs. Bidding average cost per unit would be too high for bulk stamps and too low for commemorative stamps.

The bureau's current cost accounting processes appear quite detailed and are designed to capture the costs of each of the currency note types in production in each of its printing facilities. Another, and perhaps more important, outcome of losing the stamp business was the BEP no longer considered itself indispensable. It recognized that cost effectiveness was essential to its continued existence, and this sense became ingrained in its culture. Consequently, it developed a very strong Output-Based Cost Management and Control process with two levels of monthly cost After-Action Reviews: one of which was led by the bureau director himself.

Recently, the bureau's After-Action Review processes have evolved from those described earlier (Geiger, 2011). As cost management has become more ingrained in the organization's culture, the director's Cost Review has expanded its focus into quality, spoilage, and other issues. The production cost After-Action Reviews remain robust. In fact, the bureau has added managers responsible for its products, and these managers take very active roles in the production cost After Action Reviews. Allen Wibbenmeyer, chief of the Office of Financial Management, comments:

> *Our Director's Cost Review is now more holistic and takes on more of a "balanced scorecard" approach. The cost management culture is now sufficiently engrained in the Bureau that the Production Cost Reviews work very well: especially now that we have product managers for each currency denomination that are responsible for performance of their product.*[10]

Like most federal organizations its cost accounting has also evolved into Enterprise Resource Planning (ERP), business management software. However, the bureau resisted calls to become part of a joint effort with other agencies and continued with its customized, output based design. It now uses a commercial version of Oracle ERP.

In 2014 the bureau's chief financial officer, Len Olijar, assumed the position of the director of the Bureau of Engraving and Printing. This may be the best evidence of the critical, strategic importance of cost management and control within the Bureau of Engraving and Printing.

Cost Management and Control Requirements for Success

These successful innovations demonstrated four commonalities. Each appears to be a necessary and essential requirement for success. These are leadership, staff, process, and measurement capabilities.

Aggressive and knowledgeable leadership appears to be the most important. The transition to cost management and control did not happen without sustained, active leadership. Subordinates are new to their roles and can fear the unknowns of new accountabilities. Leaders must institutionalize cost management and control quickly and prepare their inevitable successor for continued success. Continuity of leadership emphasis is also essential for a program designed for continuous improvement.

Experience has shown that while many government organizations have great leaders, those leaders have typically had little, if any, experience with cost management and control. Therefore, the second key requirement for success is *strong staff* support. Most important is an Analytic Cost Expert (ACE) who can be a change agent while making the leader cost-smart. The ACE helps the leader understand the numbers and, like a good intelligence officer, provides unbiased, mission-based observations and inputs.

Finding a good ACE was sometimes difficult. Most government accounting organizations focus on compliance with external reporting requirements and not on management support and analysis. Furthermore, many leaders have had little, if any, cost management experience and do not know what they need.

A *learning-oriented* process was present in all successful implementations. This is the cost After-Action Review. It seems to be a fundamental mechanism for constructive accountability where the focus is on fixing problems rather than on fixing blame. It must be so: Cover-up, distortion of results, and political-like spin can easily obfuscate the numbers. Blaming others and spinning the numbers are just too easy to do. The leader must create an environment in the cost After-Action Review where past performance was simply the best possible at the time and where the emphasis is placed on doing it a little better next time. This is constructive accountability.

There are only two things the leaders must expect and evaluate in the cost After-Action Review. First, subordinates must demonstrate that they understand "their" numbers. The ACE can help with this evaluation. Second, subordinates must present evidence that they are applying their knowledge and understanding by showing "their" continuous improvement initiatives. These are the changes, often creative, that inevitably result when smart people are challenged to do things a little bit better next time. It seems that there are many smart and creative people in government who have never gotten this challenge.

Actionable cost measurement is the final key requirement, but it should be clear that a control process can be based on any accounting process or methodology as long as it satisfies three requirements (Geiger, 2000). First, the reporting must be *useful* to the leader. Mind-numbing detail, very infrequent reporting, and overly aggregated numbers do not adequately support the learning objectives of the cost-review process. The second requirement is *credibility*. If no one believes the numbers, it is impossible to expect accountability. The third requirement is *affordability*. There is literally no limit to the cost that can be incurred measuring cost. It can always be done more frequently and in greater detail but quickly reaches the point of rapidly diminishing returns. Reasonable approximations may be adequate for cost management purposes, and a detailed system of direct costing may not be worth the effort. The payoffs can be significant. Even a modest 3% or 4% annual improvement in cost-effectiveness makes a big difference over a decade.

Conclusion

In conclusion, it is important to recognize that some organizations in the federal government continue to innovate with cost accounting to improve decision making and control of operations. They have achieved significant cost savings, cost avoidances, and other process improvements that have enhanced their missions. These studies into innovations in the federal government show that cost management needs good leadership, analytic staff, learning processes, and actionable cost measurement. The results of the case studies show that cost management and control is possible in the federal government and suggests that the lessons learned in their successes can benefit other government organizations seeking or needing continuous improvement in cost effectiveness.

Notes

1 FYDP: Five Year Defense Plan.
2 Author correspondence with COL Mark S. Gorak, August 10, 2015
3 General George Casey was chief of staff of the army, its highest ranking officer, from 2007 to 2011. At this time Lieutenant General Stanton was the military deputy to the assistant secretary of the army for financial management and comptroller, and Major General Marcs was the chief of army budget.
4 Training briefing by Ms. Cecile Batchelor from the Office of the Deputy Assistant Secretary of the Army for Cost and Economics at the Army Finance School, Fort Jackson, South Carolina, November 14–15, 2011.
5 Interview with Ken Graham, FORSCOM cost accounting manager, October 20, 2015.
6 Interview with Ken Graham, FORSCOM cost accounting manager, October 20, 2015. Savings and avoidances were calculated internally by comparing the cost of the alternative selected, often the "best value" alternative to the alternative with the "best" benefits
7 The resource manager on an army garrison reports to the deputy garrison commander and is responsible for all financial management and budget management functions.
8 Interview with Mike Bidelman, resource manager of Fort Belvoir, December 23, 2015.
9 Interview with Mike Bidelman, resource manager of Fort Belvoir, December 23, 2015.
10 Meeting with Allen Wibbenmeyer, chief of the Office of Financial Management, December 2, 2015.

References

Geiger, D. R. (2000). *Winning the cost war: Applying battlefield management doctrine to the management of government*. Bloomington, IN: iUniverse Star.

Geiger, D. R. (2001). Practical issues in avoiding the pitfalls in managerial costing implementation. *The Journal of Government Financial Management, 50*(1), 26–34.

Geiger, D. R. (2010). *Cost management and control in government, fighting the cost war through leadership driven management*. New York: Business Expert Press.

Martin, R. (2005). *Managerial cost accounting practices: Leadership and internal controls are key to successful implementation (GAO-05–1013R)*. Washington, DC: United States Government Accountability Office.

Martin, R. (2007). *Managerial cost accounting practices: Implementation and use vary widely across 10 federal agencies (GAO-07–679)*. Washington, DC: United States Government Accountability Office.

7 Cost Accounting in European Countries

Ringa Raudla and James W. Douglas

In the international context, cost accounting systems can be viewed as belonging to the reform package advocated by the movement of new public financial management (NPFM). NPFM refers to those aspects of new public management (NPM) that pertain to financial management (Guthrie, Olson, & Humphrey, 1999; Olson, Guthrie, & Humphrey, 1998).[1] Most generally put, NPFM is "a label for a reforming spirit intent on instilling greater 'financial awareness" into public-sector decision making (Olson et al., 1998, p. 436). Several authors have considered NPFM as constituting a key part of NPM, given that the core goals of NPM are to increase the economic efficiency and effectiveness of public-sector organizations (Flury & Schedler, 2006; Guthrie et al., 1999; Hood, 1995; Hood & Peters, 2004; ter Bogt, 2008; Torres & Pina, 2004). More specifically, NPFM includes instruments such as accrual accounting, structures to deal with the pricing and provision of public services, cost accounting systems, performance measurement, and delegated budgets (Flury & Schedler, 2006; Guthrie et al., 1999; Pina and Torres, 2003; Robbins & Lapsley, 2005; Verbeeten, 2011).

Comparative studies on NPM reforms in general and NPFM reforms in particular have pointed to rather diverse reform trajectories undertaken by different countries in Europe (Guthrie, Humphrey, Jones, & Olson, 2005; Pollitt & Bouckaert, 2004, 2011). The reform packages adopted by European governments have varied in terms of their comprehensiveness, pace, and accents (Groot & Budding, 2008; Hood, 1995; Pollitt & Bouckaert, 2004; Torres & Pina, 2004). To date, however, there are no studies that attempt to give a comprehensive overview of the utilization of cost accounting systems across European governments. While there is one study that examines cost accounting in the health sector (Tan et al., 2014), there have been no attempts to provide an overview of the use of cost accounting systems at the central government level.[2]

Our chapter is hence the first attempt to draft a preliminary "cost accounting" map of Europe. This chapter gives an overview of the use of cost accounting in the central governments of 19 European countries. Using data from a survey carried out within the framework of the largest comparative public management project undertaken in Europe to date, we provide a tentative assessment of the extent to which the different countries utilize cost accounting techniques, showing the variation in the intensity of the use of cost accounting across central government organizations. We explore the reasons that may explain the variation in the use of cost accounting between the European countries, including the role played by different administrative traditions. We also examine whether the use of cost accounting practices depends on the characteristics of the policy field, the size of the organization, and scarcity of resources. Finally, we look at whether the utilization of cost accounting systems is correlated with other NPFM practices like performance management, decentralization of financial decisions, and benchmarking.

The Data Set

The analysis employs data from the Coordinating for Cohesion in the Public Sector of the Future (COCOPS) project—one of the largest comparative public management research projects in Europe—intended to provide a comprehensive picture of the challenges facing the public sector in European countries.[3] A cornerstone of the project was the COCOPS Executive Survey on Public Sector Reform in Europe, an original, large-scale survey of public sector top executives in 19 European countries (Austria, Croatia, Denmark, Estonia, Finland, France, Germany, Hungary, Iceland, Ireland, Italy, Lithuania, the Netherlands, Norway, Portugal, Serbia, Spain, Sweden, and the UK). The survey was sent to 25,044 senior-level managers from these 19 countries, resulting in a response rate of 28.3% (7,077 valid responses). Though the survey cannot claim full representativeness for the data, it can be regarded as a good proxy and is by far the largest comparative data set for European public administrations collected up until now. In order to avoid random sampling and issues of representativeness, the COCOPS executive survey was based on a full census of all central government ministries and agencies in the target countries. It covers all high-level public-sector executives who, in their respective positions, could be expected to be involved in public administration reform processes. Generally, within all central government ministries and subordinated agencies the two top administrative levels were addressed; in some cases invitations were also sent to executives on the third level if, due to their policy relevance, this was deemed appropriate. The survey was launched in May 2012 and was implemented in several rounds (for a more detailed overview of the survey, see, e.g., Hammerschmid, Oprisor, & Stimac, 2013).

The survey aimed to explore public-sector executives' perceptions and experiences regarding public management practices, public-sector reforms, and the impact of the fiscal crisis. Our analysis focuses primarily on a subset of questions dealing specifically with respondents' perceptions of management practices within their organizations. Of particular importance for our analysis, managers were asked the extent to which cost accounting systems are used in their organizations (on a 7-point Likert scale: 1 = *Not at all*; 7 = *To a large extent*); 5,860 of the managers answered this question (82.8% of those responding to the survey).

We also utilize several other questions from the survey in order to address as thoroughly as possible the use of cost accounting across the 19 European countries. Managers were asked the extent to which (on the same 7-point scale discussed earlier) their organizations used several other management instruments: business/strategic planning, quality management systems, internal steering by contract, management by objectives and results, benchmarking, decentralization of financial decisions, performance related pay, staff appraisal/performance appraisal, and risk management. On a slightly different scale (1 = *Strongly disagree*; 7 = *Strongly agree*), managers were asked the extent to which the following statement applied to their organizations: "It is easy to observe and measure our activities." Managers were then asked to rate on a 7-point Likert scale how public administration performed over the previous 5 years within their policy areas along two dimensions: cost and efficiency and internal bureaucracy reduction/cutting red tape (1 = *Deteriorated significantly*; 7 = *Improved significantly*). Finally, managers were asked to indicate the policy area they worked within, the size of their organization, and whether they worked for a ministry or an agency or subordinate governmental body at the central government level.

The Prevalence of Cost Accounting Systems in European Central Governments: A Bird's-Eye View

Table 7.1 gives the mean responses by country to the question from the COCOPS survey asking managers the extent to which cost accounting systems are used in their organizations. The overall average of 4.37 (from the 7-point scale) indicates that cost accounting is used to a moderate extent across the 19 European countries participating in the survey. Cost accounting systems appear to be used most intensively in Sweden, the UK, Iceland, Finland, and Estonia, all with mean scores exceeding 4.85.

Figure 7.1 shows further that the top three quartiles of respondents in each of these countries scored use of cost accounting as 4 or above. In contrast, Spain and Hungary each have mean scores below 3.0, and their bottom three quartiles of respondents scored use of cost accounting as 4 or below. France, Germany, and Portugal also have relatively low mean scores (below 4.0), but as Figure 7.1 reveals, response scores in those countries are quite spread out. The remaining countries have mean scores that range from 4.08 (Lithuania) and 4.65 (Italy). What might explain some of the differences across countries?

As comparative studies on NPM in general and NPFM in particular have emphasized, the public-sector reform trajectories and the adoption of specific management instruments in different countries have been strongly influenced by contextual factors such as the existing national traditions, the

Table 7.1 Extent to Which Cost Accounting Is Used, by Country

Country	Mean	Standard Deviation	Observations
Sweden	6.00	1.34	492
United Kingdom	5.23	1.65	216
Iceland	5.13	1.84	187
Finland	4.98	1.69	652
Estonia	4.87	1.70	257
Italy	4.65	2.08	161
Denmark	4.61	1.89	127
Ireland	4.51	1.90	324
Croatia	4.50	2.01	124
Serbia	4.37	2.14	519
Austria	4.27	2.03	460
Netherlands	4.11	1.77	170
Norway	4.10	1.78	299
Lithuania	4.08	1.87	332
Portugal	3.99	2.16	212
Germany	3.81	2.05	432
France	3.19	1.98	485
Hungary	2.89	1.77	158
Spain	2.85	1.83	253
Total	**4.37**	**2.03**	**5860**

prevalent public management style, the type of administrative regime, and administrative culture (Barlow & Röber, 1996; Laughlin & Pallot, 1998; Lynn, 2006; Pollitt & Bouckaert, 2004, 2011; Torres & Pina, 2004; Verbeeten, 2011).

In the context of NPFM reforms, we can distinguish between three broad styles of public management: Anglo-Saxon, Nordic, and European Continental (Pina & Torres, 2003). Countries with the *Anglo-Saxon* style (like the UK) are more likely to adopt market-based mechanisms of public management, promote competitiveness, encourage more flexible resource allocation, and replace input controls with output controls (Pina & Torres, 2003). In terms of administrative values, pragmatism and flexibility prevail (Pollitt & Bouckaert, 2004).

Countries where the *Nordic* style dominates (Denmark, Sweden, Finland, and the Netherlands) are strongly oriented to meeting the citizens' needs, promoting decentralization and emphasizing consensus-based decision making (Pina & Torres, 2003).

The countries where the *European Continental* (or *Rechtstaat*) style predominates (e.g., France, Germany, Greece, Portugal, and Spain) are characterized by legalistic, hierarchical, and bureaucratic styles of management rooted in administrative law (Pina & Torres, 2003; Pollitt & Bouckaert, 2004, 2011).[4] In those countries, most of the civil servants are trained in law,

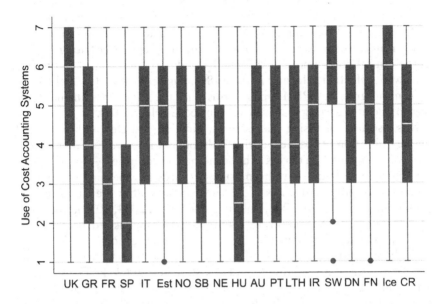

Figure 7.1 Use of Cost Accounting Systems by Country

and the core of administrative culture is rule following (Pollitt & Bouckaert, 2004, 2011). Legal compliance is valued more highly than the pursuit of efficiency, and control over inputs and processes is considered more important than control over outputs and outcomes (Gomes, Fernandes, & Carvalho, 2015; Guthrie et al., 1999). Instead of embracing NP(F)M, as Pollitt and Bouckaert (2004) point out, the administrative reform agenda in those countries could be viewed as "Neo-Weberian." On one hand, the Neo-Weberian model reaffirms the role of the state and administrative law. On the other hand, it promotes a shift from internal to external orientations for government organizations, a greater focus on citizens' needs and wishes, greater professionalization of the public service, and more results-oriented management in the use of resources (Pollitt & Bouckaert, 2004, 2011).

As our survey shows, the countries with the highest scores are Sweden, the UK, Iceland and Finland. This is certainly not a surprising finding and resonates well with existing research on NPFM reforms in European countries. In existing studies, the UK has often been designated as one of the "forerunners" of the NPM reforms in general and NPFM initiatives in particular, including the implementation of performance indicators, contracting out, delegated budgets, and accounting reforms (Barlow & Röber, 1996; Benito & Brusca, 2004; Guthrie et al., 1999; Pollitt & Bouckaert, 2004). The cost accounting reforms in the UK are probably the best known in Europe, and these have also received widespread attention in academic studies (e.g., Collier, 2006; Jackson & Lapsley, 2003; Lapsley & Wright,

2004; Liu, Michell, & Robinson, 2008; McChlery, McKendrick, & Rolfe, 2007; Van Helden, 2005). The Anglo-American style of management, with its focus on cost-consciousness, outsourcing, and accountability for outputs has certainly encouraged the implementation of cost accounting systems in the central government of the UK. Ireland, although considered to be a somewhat reluctant reformer in the 1980s, has been viewed as making significant progress in NPFM-type reforms since the mid-1990s, including the development of costing systems (Robbins & Lapsley, 2005).

It is also not surprising that Sweden, Finland, and Denmark score high on the utilization of cost accounting—although it is interesting that Sweden scores even higher than the UK. The Scandinavian countries—especially Sweden and also Finland—have been usually regarded as the runners-up in the speed and comprehensiveness of NP(F)M reforms, after the UK (Benito & Brusca, 2004; Paulsson, 2006; Pollitt & Bouckaert, 2004, 2011). The NP(F)M reforms in the Scandinavian countries have emphasized decentralized decision making (including the creation of strong agencies, independent from the ministries), and the implementation of both performance management and accrual accounting (e.g., Pina & Torres, 2003; Pollitt & Bouckaert, 2004, 2011)—all of which have certainly facilitated the adoption of cost accounting systems.[5] The decentralization initiatives in these countries have also entailed the granting of detailed decision-making authority over resource allocation to the agency level (Pollitt & Bouckaert, 2004). In Sweden, in particular, accounting issues have been at the center of public-sector reform (Guthrie et al., 1999)—which appears to be reflected in our survey results as well. It is somewhat surprising that the Netherlands—which is usually grouped together with the Nordic countries (and has also witnessed significant NPFM reforms such as accrual accounting, decentralization, and performance budgeting; Pollitt & Bouckaert, 2004, 2011; ter Bogt, 2008) scores relatively low compared to the Scandinavian countries.[6]

The list of the lowest scoring countries in our survey—Portugal, Germany, France, and Spain—does not come as a surprise either. As mentioned earlier, these countries are strongly characterized by the European Continental style of public management, rooted in administrative law. They largely have been slower—and also more selective—in adopting NP(F)M reforms. The managerialist style of management, promoted by NPM, are more difficult to advance in the more legalistic administrative systems present in these countries (Ongaro, 2009; Pina & Torres, 2003; Pollitt & Bouckaert, 2004, 2011; Torres & Pina, 2004). Spain, in particular, has been noted to "lag" behind in the NP(F)M type reforms, including cost accounting (Guthrie et al., 1999; Montesinos & Vela, 2000; Torres & Pina, 2004). In Germany, NP(F)M-style reforms—including cost calculation of administrative products, results-oriented budgeting, and decentralized resource accountability—have been adopted at the local level (Barlow & Röber, 1996; Pollitt & Bouckaert, 2004, 2011) and in the health sector (Vogl, 2012), but the federal government has been less open to them (Guthrie et al., 1999; Pollitt &

Bouckaert, 2004, 2011). In Portugal, analogously to Germany, NPFM-type reforms, including cost accounting, have been implemented at the local level (Carvalho, Gomes, & Fernandes, 2012; Pina & Torres, 2003), but the central government has been somewhat less enthusiastic in embracing them (Carvalho et al., 2012; Gomes et al., 2015).

It is noteworthy that Italy, which is often considered to belong to the Continental European group in terms of NP(F)M reforms, scores rather high on the utilization of cost accounting according to our survey. As Mussari (2005) points out, the legislative decree in 1997 foresaw cost accounting by cost centers, and this has been further developed by the ministry of finance. The Italian government has also promoted the decentralization of budgetary decisions—in the form of "frame" or "block" budgeting—as part of the overall reform package (Pollitt & Bouckaert, 2004, 2011), likely making cost accounting more useful to public managers.

In the literature on public management reform, the Central and Eastern European countries are often viewed as a distinct "group" of countries, based on their common historical heritage, and are characterized by "moderate managerialism" (Vagnoni, 2005; Verheijen & Coombes, 1998). As Vagnoni (2005) argues, these countries have, in general, been keen to displace the centralized and authoritarian political structures prevalent during the communist era and to increase their legitimacy in the eyes of the "West" by adopting management reforms that are viewed as "progressive" and "modern." Hence, they have often adopted a neoliberal and NPM-inspired mentality in their reform agendas. Our survey data, however, shows that these countries exhibit significant divergence in terms of the use of cost accounting systems. Estonia is among the high-scoring countries, Hungary is in the low-scoring group, and Croatia, Serbia, and Lithuania are in the middle.

Factors Associated With the Use of Cost Accounting Systems in European Governments

In the following, we broadly follow the perspective of the contingency theories and analyze the relationships between various organizational characteristics and the extent to which public-sector organizations in Europe use cost accounting systems. Contingency theories argue that the management practices used by organizations are influenced by their task environments, their organizational characteristics, and the technical features of their activities (Carvalho et al., 2012; Geiger & Ittner, 1996; Gordon & Miller, 1976; Chapter 1, this book).

Size

The literature suggests that larger organizations are more likely to use cost accounting (Chenhall, 2003; Chapter 2, this book; da Costa & da Costa Carvalho, 2007; Paulsson, 2006).[7] As an organization becomes larger, there is a greater need for more formal (but also sophisticated) information in order to effectively manage and coordinate organizational activities. Larger organizations tend to engage in more activities and have larger overhead costs (Mohr, 2013). Larger organizations are also likely to have more financial and analytical resources with which to adopt and implement cost accounting systems (Chenhall, 2003; da Costa & da Costa Carvalho, 2007). These attributes make use of cost accounting more probable. In their study of local governments in Portugal, da Costa and da Costa Carvalho (2007) found that larger organizations are indeed more likely to have cost accounting systems.

The responses from the COCOPS survey also indicate that larger organizations are more likely to utilize cost accounting systems. Table 7.2 shows that managers in larger organizations tend to score use of cost accounting higher as the size of their organizations increase. The overall differences between mean scores appear small, with all of the averages indicating moderate use of cost accounting. However, the means scores for organizations of fewer than 100 employees and organizations with 100 to 499 employees were both significantly less ($p < 0.01$ and 0.05, respectively) then the mean score for organizations of over 5,000 employees, providing additional evidence that size does matter when it comes to the implementation of cost accounting systems.

Policy Field

Sector-specific characteristics are considered as possible influences affecting the adoption of cost accounting systems (Groot & Budding, 2008; Hood, 1995). The COCOPS survey provides some evidence of this as well. Table 7.3 shows that managers working in the policy areas of social protection and welfare (nonhealth related) and education score use of cost accounting the highest, whereas managers working in the areas of foreign affairs and environmental protection score it the lowest. While the mean

Table 7.2 Extent to Which Cost Accounting Is Used, by Size of Organization (number of employees)

Number of Employees	Mean	Standard Deviation	Observations
<100	4.25	2.12	1,250
100 to 499	4.31	2.01	2,081
500 to 999	4.42	2.04	818
1,000 to 5,000	4.48	1.99	863
>5,000	4.58	1.94	786
Total	4.38	2.03	5798

Table 7.3 Extent to Which Cost Accounting Is Used, by Policy Area

Policy Area	Mean	Standard Deviation	Observations
Social protection and welfare (nonhealth)	4.80	1.95	298
Education	4.55	1.98	419
Multiple policy areas	4.54	1.99	871
Infrastructure and transportation	4.46	2.02	375
General government	4.43	2.09	618
Recreation, culture, religion	4.38	2.10	204
Defense	4.36	1.85	130
Finance	4.35	2.03	468
Employment services	4.34	2.01	394
Health	4.33	2.00	339
Justice, public order & safety	4.32	2.05	535
Economic affairs	4.21	2.03	441
Environmental protection	4.16	2.04	273
Other	4.12	2.12	303
Foreign affairs	3.64	2.00	192
Total	4.37	2.03	5,860

scores vary across policy areas, there are no clear reasons why this is the case. No distinct patterns emerge from the table. What is it about policy areas such as social protection and welfare that make them more likely than others, such as foreign affairs, to utilize cost accounting systems? Future research is needed to address this question.

Measurability of Tasks

According to the contingency theory, discussed in Chapter 2 of this book, task complexity is likely to influence the use of cost accounting. Based on the existing literature, we can expect that the more easily measurable the activities of the organization, the more feasible the adoption of cost accounting measures (Carvalho et al., 2012; Cavalluzzo & Ittner, 2004; Chenhall, 2003; Doyle, Duffy, & McCahey, 2008; Olson, Humphrey, & Guthrie, 2001). Responses to the COCOPS survey suggest that this is true to at least some degree. We ran a bivariate correlation between responses to the cost accounting question and managers' responses to the question asking the extent to which it is easy to observe and measure their organization's activities. The resulting correlation coefficient was 0.2397 (significant at the $p < 0.001$ level). While the association is not particularly strong, it does indicate that cost accounting systems are indeed utilized more in organizations where the measurability of tasks is relatively easier.

Agency Versus Ministry

On one hand, the literature suggest that agencies are more likely to use cost accounting than ministries because they are more directly involved in the provision of services (rather than policy making; Van Helden, 2005). On the other hand, when the agencies are subordinated to the ministries, it is possible that the ministries will use cost accounting for evaluating the activities of their agencies (Paulsson, 2006). The responses to the COCOPS survey suggest that the former proposition is more accurate. Managers working at the ministry level generated a mean score of 3.77 for use of cost accounting systems, indicating relatively low usage. In contrast, the mean score for respondents working at the agency level was 4.90, significantly higher ($p <$ 0.001) than the score for the ministries. As a result, it appears that cost accounting methods are particularly useful for units engaged more closely in service provision.

Scarcity of Resources

The *scarcity of resources* and the goal to drive down the costs are likely to play an important role in spurring the adoption of cost accounting systems (Carvalho et al., 2012; Jackson & Lapsley, 2003; Mohr, 2013; Verbeeten, 2011). Cost management systems like cost accounting can help politicians and managers to reduce costs and improve the allocation of resources (Carvalho et al., 2012; Geiger & Ittner, 1996; Mohr, 2013; Verbeeten, 2011). This has been observed as one of the motivators of NPM reforms, in general (Hood, 1995; Pollitt & Bouckaert, 2011; Raudla, Randma-Liiv, & Savi, 2015; ter Bogt, 2008; Torres & Pina, 2004), and NPFM reforms, in particular (Benito & Brusca, 2004; Carvalho et al., 2012; Raudla, 2013; Raudla et al., 2015). It was hoped that the adoption of NPM instruments would help to cut expenditures and curtail budget deficits (Carvalho et al., 2012; Osborne & Gaebler, 1992; Pollitt & Bouckaert, 2004). Cost accounting systems can provide information about what drives the costs in organizations and thus help to decide where cutbacks could fall (Mohr, 2013). Cost accounting systems can also help to indicate which services are provided inefficiently (relative to similar services) and could point to possibilities for productivity improvements (Mohr, 2013). On the other hand, the implementation of cost accounting systems themselves may entail significant expenditures (Al-Omiri & Drury, 2007; Doyle et al., 2008; Mohr, 2013, 2016; Olson et al., 2001), and in the presence of squeezed resources, organizations may be reluctant to adopt such systems. Lapsley and Wright (2004), in their study of public-sector organizations in Scotland, observe that ABC is more likely to be used when it is necessary to tightly control expenditures. Similarly, a number of studies about the private sector have pointed to increased *scarcity of resources* as a driver behind the adoption of management accounting innovations like cost accounting (Lin & Yu, 2002; Reid & Smith, 2000).

The COCOPS survey does not address the motivations behind adopting cost accounting systems directly. However, if governments were motivated by resource scarcity issues, then we would expect the use of cost accounting to be associated with cost reduction efforts and improved efficiency. Fortunately, two questions in the survey asked managers to assess how their policy areas performed in dealing with "cost and efficiency" and "internal bureaucracy reduction/cutting red tape." Responses to both of these questions were positively correlated with responses regarding the use of cost accounting systems. The correlation coefficients were 0.2071 ($p < 0.001$) for "cost and efficiency" and 0.1353 ($p < 0.001$) for "internal bureaucracy reduction/cutting red tape." Thus, the more useful a respondent indicated that cost accounting systems were in their organizations, the more likely they were to perceive improvements in these two areas; although the association is stronger for cost and efficiency than it is for cuts to bureaucracy, perhaps indicating that cost accounting is a better tool for detecting areas for potential productivity gains than for identifying areas for possible cuts.

Correlations With Other Management Instruments

Cost accounting systems may play an important role in providing useful informational inputs for the functioning of other management instruments promoted by NP(F)M, especially performance management and benchmarking (Evans & Bellamy, 1995; Flury & Schedler, 2006; Johnson & Kaplan, 1991; Rivenbark & Carter, 2000; Turney, 2010; Verbeeten, 2011).[8] For example, cost accounting systems can provide information for the calculation of *efficiency* measures—rather than just *output* measures—in performance measurement systems (Mohr, 2013, 2016; Rivenbark, 2005). Especially when the ABC format is used, the cost accounting system can be the very source of performance measures (Turney, 2010). Information generated by cost accounting systems can enable managers to evaluate unit costs in order to make resource allocation decisions—for example, rewarding units that are more effective with additional resources (Mohr, 2016). Cost accounting systems can also offer valuable information for undertaking benchmarking. The broader estimates of costs for identical services provide more comparable and standardized information for benchmarking—allowing managers to evaluate more accurately and transparently the efficiency of their organizations (Flury & Schedler, 2006; Mohr, 2016). ABC, in particular, can be used to generate metrics that are needed for meaningful benchmarking (Doyle et al., 2008; Mohr, 2013, 2016). In addition to complementarities with performance management and benchmarking, decentralized organizational structures can be expected to promote the use of cost accounting (Chenhall, 2003; Mohr, Chapter 1 of this book; Olson et al., 2001; Verbeeten, 2011).

Table 7.4 reveals that many management instruments are being used across the 19 European countries included in the COCOPS survey. Interestingly, fewer respondents made an assessment regarding cost accounting

Table 7.4 Extent to Which Various Management Instruments Are Used

Management Instruments	Mean	Standard Deviation	Observations
Cost accounting systems	4.37	2.03	5860
Staff appraisal talks/ performance appraisal	5.51***	1.76	6533
Business/strategic planning	5.39***	1.61	6647
Management by objective and results	5.29***	1.72	6625
Risk management	4.38	1.95	6262
Quality management systems	4.34	1.91	6387
Benchmarking	4.16***	1.86	6354
Internal steering by contract	4.07***	2.10	5915
Decentralization of financial decisions	3.76***	1.90	6004
Performance related pay	3.13***	2.05	6611

***Significantly different from *cost accounting systems* at the .001 level.

systems than for any other management instrument. This may indicate unfamiliarity with cost accounting among many managers, causing them to skip the question in the survey. The table also shows that managers perceive performance appraisals, strategic planning, and management by objectives and results to be used to a greater extent than cost accounting systems. In contrast, benchmarking, internal steering by contract, decentralized financial decision making, and performance related pay are perceived to be used significantly less.

Table 7.5 shows the extent to which the uses of the various management instruments are correlated with use of cost accounting systems. As posited by the literature, the use of cost accounting is strongly correlated with benchmarking and performance management techniques and decentralized decision-making structures. In fact, the use of cost accounting is at least moderately correlated with all of the management instruments listed in the table. This is possibly due to larger efforts by managers to improve their decision making by modernizing their management systems and enhancing the quality of information available to them—managers seeking to make such improvements are likely to adopt multiple methods to achieve this goal. The associations we identify in Table 7.5, however, leave an important question left unanswered. While our survey findings indicate that the use

Table 7.5 Bivariate Correlations of Use of Cost Accounting With Other Management Instruments

Management Instruments	Correlation Coefficients (N)
Decentralization of financial decisions	0.4651*** (5,500)
Risk management	0.4553*** (5,531)
Benchmarking	0.4249*** (5,583)
Business/strategic planning	0.4169*** (5,688)
Management by objectives and results	0.4161*** (5,661)
Quality management systems	0.3850*** (5,574)
Internal steering by contract	0.3293*** (5,270)
Staff appraisal talks/performance appraisal	0.3250*** (5,571)
Performance-related pay	0.3071*** (5,714)

Note. Number of observations in parenthesis.

***Significant at the .001 level.

of cost accounting is indeed correlated with the use of other management instruments, our data do not allow us to examine to what extent the information supplied by cost accounting systems actually influences or provides input for the other management practices.[9] This should be the subject of future research.

Concluding Remarks

This chapter is a first attempt to give a comparative overview of the use of cost accounting systems in the central governments of European countries. None of the existing comparative studies on NPFM reforms has focused explicitly on cost accounting systems. The survey data from the COCOPS project, covering 19 countries, indicates that there is variation between the European countries with regard to the utilization of cost accounting systems. Cost accounting systems appear to be used most intensively in Sweden, the UK, Iceland, Finland, and Estonia and least intensively in Spain, Hungary, France, Germany, and Portugal. The countries of Italy, Denmark, Ireland, Croatia, Serbia, Austria, the Netherlands, Norway, and Lithuania fall between these two groups. These results are pretty much in line with the findings of other comparative studies, which have pointed to the UK and the Scandinavian countries as the frontrunners in NPFM reforms. The survey findings indicate that the use of cost accounting systems seems to be facilitated by Anglo-Saxon and Scandinavian administrative cultures, with their focus on efficiency and decentralization, respectively. In contrast, the countries where the European Continental style of administration dominates (with its focus on the rule of law and legal compliance), cost accounting systems are used less often.

In addition to "drawing" a preliminary cost accounting map of Europe, we explored whether different organizational variables are associated with the use of cost accounting systems. In line with the expectations of contingency theories, we found that organizational size, the measurability of organizations' activities, and increased scarcity of resources are indeed correlated with more extensive use of cost accounting. Finally, we can observe that at the organizational level, the use of cost accounting systems is significantly correlated with the use of other management instruments advocated by NP(F)M, especially with performance management, benchmarking, and decentralization of financial decisions.

In interpreting these results, it is important, however, to keep in mind that the data from the COCOPS survey are limited in that we rely on the perceptions of managers. Furthermore, the question about the use of cost accounting systems was very general and no information was collected about the *type(s)* of cost accounting systems. We therefore know little about the details of the cost accounting systems used in the European countries covered in this chapter. We believe, however, that this chapter provides a good starting point for future comparative studies that can explore the use of cost accounting systems in more depth.

Notes

1 The NPM doctrine includes the promotion of the implementation of the following reforms and management instruments in the public sector: the promotion of greater competition in the public sector, the focus on managerial accountability, hands-on professional management, stress on discipline and frugality in resource use, downsizing, privatization, outsourcing, the development of performance management and measurement systems, replacement of input controls with output controls, and decentralization (Guthrie et al., 1999; Hood, 1995; Hood & Peters, 2004; Osborne & Gaebler, 1992; Pollitt & Bouckaert, 2004; Torres & Pina, 2004).

2 Van Helden (2005) has observed that the literature on management accounting focuses primarily on reforms either at the local government level or in the health care sector rather than at the central government level. This may be because these sectors are more open to management accounting reforms and generally more innovative in experimenting with public management reforms (Guthrie et al., 1999) or because they deal with more specific services compared to many central government organizations (Van Helden, 2005).

3 The research leading to these results has received funding from the European Union's Seventh Framework Programme under grant agreement No. 266887 (Project COCOPS) Socio-economic Sciences and Humanities. For more detailed information, see www.cocops.eu.

4 In the literature, more detailed taxonomies of the European Continental administrative style have often been put forth. Some authors distinguish between the Germanic and Southern European (or Napoleonic) styles (Painter & Peters, 2010; Pollitt & Bouckaert, 2011; Torres & Pina, 2004).

5 Especially Sweden and Finland stand out for the number of independent agencies that have been created (Pina & Torres, 2003).

6 Verbeeten (2011) has also observed that ABC is not used on a widespread scale in the Dutch public sector; instead, most of the organizations prefer the "German/Dutch cost pool method" to allocate costs.

7 In the private-sector context, the studies point to diverging findings: Libby and Waterhouse (1996) found that organizational size was not significant in predicting the adoption of changes in management accounting systems. Brown, Booth, and Giacobbe (2004) and Krumwiede (1998), however, found that organizational size did influence the adoption of ABC, with larger organizations being more likely to adopt.

8 An alternative perspective states that cost accounting may compete with performance management systems (Mohr, 2016). First, cost accounting systems may make managers focus more on inputs and processes, at the expense of outputs of outcomes. Second, the development of more sophisticated cost accounting systems (like ABC) requires extensive resources, which may compete with the resources needed for performance information systems. (Mohr, 2016)

9 As Verbeeten (2011) has shown, cost management systems may be adopted by organizations in order to satisfy external pressures, but they make only limited use of the information provided. Institutionalist literature (especially sociological institutionalism) has argued that management reforms and organizational changes may be adopted in order to enhance organizational legitimacy, without the practices having significant bearing on organizational decision making (Carvalho et al., 2012; DiMaggio & Powell, 1991; Geiger & Ittner, 1996; Johansson & Siverbo, 2009; ter Bogt, 2008).

References

Al-Omiri, M., & Drury, C. (2007). Organizational and behavioral factors influencing the adoption and success of ABC in the UK. *Journal of Cost Management*, 21(6), 38–48.

Barlow, J., & Röber, M. (1996). Steering not rowing: Co-ordination and control in the management of public services in Britain and Germany. *International Journal of Public Sector Management*, 9(5–6), 73–89.

Benito, B., & Brusca, I. (2004). International classification of local government accounting systems. *Journal of Comparative Policy Analysis: Research and Practice*, 6(1), 57–80.

Brown, D. A., Booth, P., & Giacobbe, F. (2004). Technological and organizational influences on the adoption of activity-based costing in Australia. *Accounting and Finance*, 44(3), 329–356.

Carvalho, J. B. D. C., Gomes, P. S., & José Fernandes, M. (2012). The main determinants of the use of the cost accounting system in Portuguese local government. *Financial Accountability & Management*, 28(3), 306–334.

Cavalluzzo, K. S., & Ittner, C. D. (2004). Implementing performance measurement innovations: Evidence from government. *Accounting, Organizations and Society*, 29(3), 243–267.

Chenhall, R. (2003). Management control systems design within its organizational context: Findings from contingency-based research and directions for the future. *Accounting, Organizations and Society*, 28(2–3), 127–168.

Collier, P. M. (2006). Costing police services: The politicization of accounting. *Critical Perspectives on Accounting*, 17(1), 57–86.

da Costa, T. D. C. S., & da Costa Carvalho, J. B. (2007). Cost accounting applications in local governments: The case of municipal tariff and price setting in the north of Portugal. *Revista Contemporânea de Contabilidade*, 1(7), 11–24.

DiMaggio, P., & Powell, W. W. (1991). The iron cage revisited: Institutional isomorphism and collective rationality in organizational fields. In W. W. Powell &

P. Dimaggio (Eds.), *The new institutionalism in organizational analysis* (pp. 63–82). Chicago, IL: University of Chicago Press.

Doyle, G., Duffy, L., & McCahey, M. (2008). *An empirical study of adoption/nonadoption of activity based costing in hospitals in Ireland.* UCD Business Schools Working Paper, 1–43.

Evans, P., & Bellamy, S. (1995). Performance evaluation in the Australian public sector: The role of management and cost accounting control systems. *International Journal of Public Sector Management, 8*(6), 30–38.

Flury, R., & Schedler, K. (2006). Political versus managerial use of cost and performance accounting. *Public Money and Management, 26*(4), 229–234.

Geiger, D. R., & Ittner, C. D. (1996). The influence of funding source and legislative requirements on government cost accounting practices. *Accounting, Organizations and Society, 21*(6), 549–567.

Gomes, P. S., Fernandes, M. J., & Carvalho, J. B. D. C. (2015). The international harmonization process of public sector accounting in Portugal: The perspective of different stakeholders. *International Journal of Public Administration, 38*(4), 268–281.

Gordon, L. A., & Miller, D. (1976). A contingency framework for the design of accounting information systems. *Accounting, Organizations and Society, 1*(1), 59–69.

Groot, T., & Budding, T. (2008). New public management's current issues and future prospects. *Financial Accountability & Management, 24*(1), 1–13.

Guthrie, J., Humphrey, C., Jones, L. R., & Olson, O. (Eds.) (2005). *International public financial management reform.* Charlotte, NC: Information Age Publishing.

Guthrie, J., Olson, O., & Humphrey, C. (1999). Debating developments in new public financial management: The limits of global theorising and some new ways forward. *Financial Accountability & Management, 15*(3–4), 209–228.

Hammerschmid, G., Oprisor, A., & Stimac, V. (2013). *COCOPS executive survey on public sector reform in Europe: Research report.* Retrieved from http://www.cocops.eu/wp-content/uploads/2013/06/COCOPS-WP3-Research-Report.pdf

Hood, C. (1995). The "New Public Management" in the 1980s: Variations on a theme. *Accounting, Organizations and Society, 20*(2), 93–109.

Hood, C., & Peters, G. (2004). The middle aging of new public management: Into the age of paradox? *Journal of Public Administration Research and Theory, 14*(63), 267–282.

Jackson, A., & Lapsley, I. (2003). The diffusion of accounting practices in the new "managerial" public sector. *International Journal of Public Sector Management, 16*(5), 359–372.

Johansson, T., & Siverbo, S. (2009). Explaining the utilization of relative performance evaluation in local government: A multi-theoretical study using data from Sweden. *Financial Accountability & Management, 25*(2), 197–224.

Johnson, H. T., & Kaplan, R. S. (1991). *Relevance lost: The rise and fall of management accounting.* Boston, MA: Harvard Business Press.

Krumwiede, K. R. (1998). The implementation stages of activity-based costing and the impact of contextual and organizational factors. *Journal of Management Accounting Research, 10*(2), 293–27.

Lapsley, I., & Wright, E. (2004). The diffusion of management accounting innovations in the public sector: A research agenda. *Management Accounting Research, 15*(3), 355–374.

Laughlin, R., & Pallot, J. (1998). Trends, patterns and influencing factors: Some reflections. In O. Olson, J. Guthrie, & C. Humphrey (Eds.), *Global warning: Debating international developments in new public financial management* (pp. 376–399). Oslo: Cappelen Akademisk Folag.

Libby, T., & Waterhouse, J. H. (1996). Predicting change in management accounting systems. *Journal of Management Accounting Research, 8*(1), 137.

Lin, Z. J., & Yu, Z. (2002). Responsibility cost control system in China: A case of management accounting application. *Management Accounting Research, 13*(4), 447–467.

Liu, Y. J. L., Mitchell, F., & Robinson, J. (2008). A longitudinal study of the adoption of an activity-based planning system in the crown prosecution service of England and Wales, United Kingdom. *Journal of Accounting & Organizational Change, 4*(3), 318–342.

Lynn, L. (2006). *Public management: Old and new.* New York: Routledge.

McChlery, S., McKendrick, J., & Rolfe, T. (2007). Activity-based management systems in higher education. *Public Money and Management, 27*(5), 315–322.

Mohr, Z. T. (2013). *Cost accounting in U.S. cities: Transition costs and governance factors affecting cost accounting development and use.* Dissertation: University of Kansas.

Mohr, Z. T. (2016). Performance measurement and cost accounting: Are they complementary or competing systems of control? *Public Administration Review, 76*(4), 616–625.

Montesinos, V., & Vela, J. M. (2000). Governmental accounting in Spain and the European Monetary Union: A critical perspective. *Financial Accountability & Management, 16*(2), 129–150.

Mussari, R. (2005). Public sector financial management reform in Italy. In J. Guthrie, C. Humphrey, & L. R. Jones (Eds.), *International public financial management reform: Progress, contradictions, and challenges* (pp. 139–168). Charlotte, NC: Information Age Publishing.

Olson, O., Guthrie, J., & Humphrey, C. (1998). Growing accustomed to other faces: The global themes and warnings of our project. In O. Olson, J. Guthrie, & C. Humphrey (Eds.), *Global warning: Debating international developments in new public financial management* (pp. 435–466). Oslo: Cappelen Akademisk Forlag AS.

Olson, O., Humphrey, C., & Guthrie, J. (2001). Caught in an evaluatory trap: A dilemma for public services under NPFM. *European Accounting Review, 10*(3), 505–522.

Ongaro, E. (2009). *Public management reform and modernization: Trajectories of administrative change in Italy, France, Greece, Portugal and Spain.* Cheltenham and Northampton: Edward Elgar.

Osborne, D., & Gaebler, T. (1992). *Reinventing government: How the entrepreneurial spirit is transforming government.* New York: Plume Books.

Painter, M., & Peters, G. B. (2010). *Tradition and public administration.* Basingstoke: Palgrave Macmillan.

Paulsson, G. (2006). Accrual accounting in the public sector: Experiences from the central government in Sweden. *Financial Accountability & Management, 22*(1), 47–62.

Pina, V., & Torres, L. (2003). Reshaping public sector accounting: An international comparative view. *Canadian Journal of Administrative Sciences, 20*(4), 334–350.

Pollitt, C., & Bouckaert, G. (2004). *Public management reform: A comparative analysis*. Oxford: Oxford University Press.

Pollitt, C., & Bouckaert, G. (2011). *Public management reform: A comparative analysis—new public management, governance and the Neo-Weberian state*. Oxford: Oxford University Press.

Raudla, R. (2013). Budgeting during austerity: Approaches, instruments and practices. *Budgetary Research Review*, 5(1), 30–39.

Raudla, R., Randma-Liiv, T., & Savi, R. (2015). Public sector financial and personnel management during cutbacks: Looking back at the literature of the 1970s and 1980s. *Administrative Culture*, 16(2), 117–140.

Reid, G. C., & Smith, J. A. (2000). The impact of contingencies on management accounting system development. *Management Accounting Research*, 11(4), 427–450.

Rivenbark, W. C. (2005). A historical overview of cost accounting in local government. *State & Local Government Review*, 37(3), 217–227.

Rivenbark, W. C., & Carter, K. L. (2000). Benchmarking and cost accounting: The North Carolina approach. *Journal of Public Budgeting Accounting and Financial Management*, 12(1), 125–137.

Robbins, G., & Lapsley, I. (2005). NPM and the Irish public sector: From reluctant reformer to statutory codification. In J. Guthrie, C. Humphrey, & L. R. Jones (Eds.), *International public financial management reform: Progress, contradictions, and challenges* (pp. 109–138). Charlotte, NC: Information Age Publishing.

Tan, S. S., Geissler, A., Serdén, L., Heurgren, M., van Ineveld, B. M., Redekop, W. K., & Hakkaart-van Roijen, L. (2014). DRG systems in Europe: Variations in cost accounting systems among 12 countries. *The European Journal of Public Health*, 24(6), 1023–1028.

ter Bogt, H. J. (2008). Management accounting change and new public management in local government: A reassessment of ambitions and results—an institutionalist approach to accounting change in the Dutch public sector. *Financial Accountability & Management*, 24(3), 209–241.

Torres, L., & Pina, V. (2004). Reshaping public administration: The Spanish experience compared to the UK. *Public Administration*, 82(2), 445–464.

Turney, P. B. (2010). Activity-based costing: An emerging foundation for performance management. *Cost Management*, 24(4), 33.

Vagnoni, E. (2005). Eastern European nations and new public financial management. In J. Guthrie, C. Humphrey, & L. R. Jones (Eds.), *International public financial management reform: Progress, contradictions, and challenges* (pp. 87–107). Charlotte, NC: Information Age Publishing.

Van Helden, G. J. (2005). Researching public sector transformation: The role of management accounting. *Financial Accountability & Management*, 21(1), 99–133.

Verbeeten, F. H. (2011). Public sector cost management practices in The Netherlands. *International Journal of Public Sector Management*, 24(6), 492–506.

Verheijen, T., & Coombes, D. L. (Eds.) (1998). *Innovations in public management: Perspectives from East and West Europe*. Cheltenham: Edward Elgar Publishing.

Vogl, M. (2012). Assessing DRG cost accounting with respect to resource allocation and tariff calculation: The case of Germany. *Health Economics Review*, 2(1), 1–12.

8 Extending the Application and Theory of Government Cost Accounting

Zachary T. Mohr

This book began by arguing that government cost accounting was important both practically and theoretically. In many ways, it has shown the important applications of cost accounting in different organizational areas: accounting (Chapter 5), performance (Chapter 3), pricing (Chapter 4), and management (Chapter 6). These chapters represent a snapshot and empirical base for building out descriptive and theoretical research. In this last chapter, extensions for theory and practice are drawn. Extensions are discussed that are currently happening or that should be encouraged to happen. While government cost accounting research has been limited in recent years, the longevity of the practice and the forces at work in our organizational world suggest that it will remain a relevant topic for the foreseeable future. The chapter first discusses the extensions of applications that are both needed for practice and theory development. It then discusses extensions for theory that can help build a basis for government cost accounting research. Finally, it discusses the need to bridge practice and theory and how this may be encouraged.

Extending Cost Accounting Applications and Practices

In Chapter 2 it was shown that cost accounting was first about accounting and budgeting. In the beginning of the 20th century, basic types of activity analysis were used to determine the elements that were needed in early government budget documents. It was then advocated as a tool of budgeting. Today, cost accounting is directly connected to government accounting for grants. Eger and McDonald (Chapter 5) show that grant cost accounting is not standing still. Recent executive orders have encouraged streamlining the guidance on cost accounting and promoting the direction of resources to evidence-based outcomes. Unfortunately, this order and the previous regulations in the federal register largely just reiterate what was codified in the OMB cost accounting circulars (A-21, A-87, and A-122). In reality, little progress has been made in the costing principles that the United States federal government requires of grantee governments, universities, and non-profits in recent decades. While streamlining the regulations and making cost accounting more evidence based should be encouraged, it needs to be recognized that grant cost accounting is now more than a half century old, and many of the systems and practices have evolved due to the unique challenges of cost accounting in a highly differentiated organizational environment. More research should be done in this area before policy makers try to make significant changes to the system.

Additionally, the GASB abandoned cost accounting standards in the 1960s. It now allows indirect costs to be included in the government-wide financial statements, but no one has ever researched why some governments choose to give indirect cost information in their financial statements or what impact this has on financial or organizational outcomes. FASAB has not updated it costing standard since the 1990s. Standard setting bodies should be encouraged to research cost accounting and modify standards or provide guidance where appropriate.

Performance measurement and management seems to be the logical direction for cost accounting to be developed. Rivenbark and Mohr (Chapter 2) show that cost accounting has been most closely associated with performance management in recent years. Rivenbark (Chapter 3) provides the logical foundations for the connection between cost accounting and performance measures in benchmarking regimes. While Rivenbark discussed the successful North Carolina Benchmarking Project, other notable government benchmarking systems do not use cost accounting to develop estimates of resources consumed when establishing benchmarks (Coe, 1999). Other important performance measurement concepts like Balanced Scorecards (BSC) and Total Quality Management (TQM) are also importantly connected to cost accounting (Chapter 6), but there is a general dearth of examples in the government accounting literature that has discussed the connection between the tools of BSC or TQM and cost accounting systems in government. The development of systems similar to the North Carolina project should be encouraged, as should successful examples of BSC and TQM that have used cost accounting to achieve different or better effects.

That cost accounting is connected to performance management suggests that cost accounting is more than an accounting system or practice. Cost accounting is equally a tool of management and strategy. Geiger (Chapter 6) showed how the federal government has utilized cost accounting in several areas to improve management decision making. Pope and Mohr (Chapter 4) discussed how different pricing arrangements can be used in public organizations to change citizen, consumer behavior, but these pricing decisions may need to be justified on a cost basis. Ultimately, where we draw the cost boundaries or establish the cost objective can greatly influence the perception of cost. Governments and cost analysts often need to decide which of a multitude of costs that they need to look at. These costs will be determined based on the strategy the government or government leaders are following. As such, it should be noted that cost accounting is related to strategy, and it should be studied within public administration and management fields as well as in accounting fields. Unfortunately today, too many public administration students have very little idea at all about cost accounting as they are only briefly exposed to it in a budget or financial management class. The administration and management field needs to recognize and teach core principles of cost accounting to all students. Key parts of the curriculum where this could be taught are in courses or classes that are discussing performance or grants. Ultimately, cost accounting concepts can be applied more extensively in many areas that could greatly benefit from a consideration of all the resources needed to produce a good or service for citizens, consumers, or the public, in general.

Extending Cost Accounting Theory

Recognizing that cost accounting is a topic that is relevant to more than just accounting and government accountants is very important for theory development. Management theories and topics that are of interest to management are important, as are theories of politics and sociology because the topic of government cost spills over into our social life and politics (Collier, 2006).

While most of the literature on business cost accounting systems and some on government cost accounting has taken a contingency theoretic perspective (Chapter 1), government cost accounting could benefit greatly from several broad theoretical and research traditions. Raudla and Douglas (Chapter 7) provide a descriptive and contingency theory analysis of cost accounting practices in Europe based upon the NPM frame. Comparative work that looks at cost accounting differences in Europe is an important stream of research (i.e., Carvalho, Gomes, & José Fernandes, 2012; Ter Bogt, 2008; Verbeeten, 2011), but comparisons between costing practices in Europe with practices in the United States that was not as heavily influenced by NPM could be very informative on the role that large social movements play in influencing these microlevel tools and practices. Additionally, behavioral theories and behavioral approaches should be followed to answer questions such as what impact different cost information has on the decisions of managers, legislators, and the opinion of the public. Finally, theories of conflict and implementation challenges need to be pursued because cost accounting is not used nearly as extensively as its many purposes suggests it could be used (Mohr, 2015).

Government cost accounting theory development is greatly hampered by its lack of a solid definition. Many definitions in the field either reject government as capable of cost accounting[1] or focus too narrowly on specific aspects like its purpose (i.e., informing management decisions). In government, cost accounting is used for many purposes and has many audiences. It is not appropriate to claim that government cost accounting only informs management decisions,[2] but it also informs higher levels of government (Chapter 5), the courts (Chapter 4), and the public at large (Chapter 3). Therefore, a new definition of cost accounting is needed.

This research provides the basis or the beginnings of what a good definition of government cost accounting might look like. A key part of that definition is that cost accounting provides a broader definition of cost besides just the direct costs but includes all of the resources (direct, indirect, and capital; see Chapters 1 and 3 for more detail) that are needed for service delivery. Importantly, these resources cross organizational and budgetary boundaries. For example, the resource estimate used for the benchmarks in Chapter 3 include resources from different parts of the organization's budget. Cost accounting also includes indirect and support center costs for grants (Chapter 5) and for rates (Chapter 4). Both of these involve the tracking of costs across boundaries within the organization for justification across the organizational boundary to either higher levels of government or to citizens. Finally, Geiger (Chapter 6) shows that managers can also use these same cost accounting principles to better manage resources across the departmental boundaries of the organization. All of these examples suggest that cost accounting is the calculation and management of organizational resources across boundaries. This definition is important because it draws attention to the general features and the ubiquity of cost accounting practices in modern organizations. Nearly all modern organizations have multiple departments and many types of indirect costs such as human resources, IT, accounting and administration just to name a few. The recognition that different parts of the organization consume disproportionate amounts of these indirect resources drives the need to study these costs, especially when the costs are large. Shifting the focus to services that are consuming resources across boundaries suggests the likely areas where cost accounting is likely to be important both theoretically and in practice.

The definition is also important because it points to the extension of cost accounting into the financial management across organizations. Already cost accounting is recognized as important for contracts between government and the private sector. What is less often recognized is that cost accounting is also important for the financial management of collaborations such as a fire department providing service in another community or providing joint service through an interlocal agreement. This networked service provision has a variety of technical and political challenges surrounding the establishment of costs and price that simply have not been discussed in sufficient detail, largely because there is a dearth of literature on cost accounting in government organizations. There are a few examples of early research projects on cost accounting in collaborative network setting such as Mohr and Mitchell's (2014) analysis of indirect cost monitoring in Chicago local governments or studies of public health services like substance abuse costs that have both direct and indirect costs from multiple agencies (Zarkin, Dunlap, & Homsi, 2004). Both of these studies found that cost accounting importantly influences the estimate and perception of cost for these services. Once it is realized that cost accounting concepts and principles are more generalizable than common definitions suggest, it becomes readily apparent that many of these concepts are relevant in many other areas of practice and may be important to study in light of other theories.

Conclusion: Bridging Theory and Practice

It seems that one of the key impediments to both the development of the theory and applications of government cost accounting is simply a dearth of thoughtful analysis on the topic. This impediment will take care of itself if more research on the topic is published. However, some logistical challenges still remain to getting a government cost accounting research agenda established. Most important, there are semantic challenges to cost accounting research. When citizens say, "Government cost," they are often asking, "What is the price, or what is it going to cost me?" The broader definition of cost accounting suggests that cost accounting is about resource use across boundaries and that this estimate is dependent on the cost objective of the analysis. This estimate of cost may be very different than the estimate of cost relevant to the citizen. Likewise, other key terms have multiple meanings. Sometimes a finance or budget official may say that they are doing ABC when they mean that they are doing cost accounting or hybrid costing as was discussed in Chapter 1. When asked about indirect costs, managers may be referring to direct costs that are simply not usually included in the estimate of the cost because these direct costs are in the accounting system in some other part of the organization. In all manner of cost research, it becomes important to determine what is meant when government finance practitioners are interviewed or surveyed. It also becomes important to remember that the practitioners have good reason for referring to the cost or the system as they have. Another term that is often thrown out by practitioners is *full cost accounting*, which may have multiple meanings. What is often meant by practitioners, though, is a fuller cost of service than just the usual direct costs or expenses. There is great frustration among some practitioners that they see these concepts as important, but there is not research being done on the topic because the research community cannot get behind an analysis simply because academics cannot understand if practitioners mean a full and marginal cost or whether it is a full cost that mixes fixed and marginal costs. If it matters to practitioners enough to do it, it should matter enough to study the subject and its consequences. It is incumbent upon the researcher and the research community to try to understand what is meant and what the implications are from practitioners' answers that may not fit into common definitions of cost accounting or economics. In other words, research should not be discouraged simply because practitioners have used terms loosely if it can be shown that interesting and important relationships exist either practically or theoretically.

Another way to encourage research in government cost accounting is to encourage publication in practitioner journals, especially by practitioners, about cost accounting concepts. Journals such as the *Government*

Accountants Journal have published important work on government cost accounting in the United States (i.e., Geiger, 2001; Kennett, Durler, & Downs, 2007) that kept the discussion of government cost accounting moving forward in the United States when academics were not publishing on the subject.

Finally, cost accounting has been shown to be importantly connected for both practical and theoretical reasons to some of the hottest topics in accounting and management. Connections and studies of cost accounting should be pursued in areas such as performance management, contract management, and collaboration. All of these fields can benefit from more information about how cost accounting can change the perspective and the discussion. Ultimately, cost accounting remains important for core aspects of government such as grants and rate setting, but it is also poised to importantly contribute to the discussion and research of many other significant areas of government accounting and management.

Notes

1 For example, the Google search definition of *cost accounting* is "the recording of all the costs incurred *in a business* in a way that can be used to improve its management." Retrieved 7/15/2016.
2 It can inform management in government, too. This is shown in Chapters 3 and 6, but it is used for more than just management decision making in government.

References

Carvalho, J. B. D. C., Gomes, P. S., & José Fernandes, M. (2012). The main determinants of the use of the cost accounting system in Portuguese local government. *Financial Accountability & Management, 28*(3), 306–334.

Coe, C. (1999). Local government benchmarking: Lessons from two major multi-government efforts. *Public Administration Review, 59*(2), 110–123.

Collier, P. M. (2006). Costing police services: The politicization of accounting. *Critical Perspectives on Accounting, 17*(1), 57–86.

Geiger, D. R. (2001). Practical issues in avoiding the pitfalls in managerial costing implementation. *The Journal of Government Financial Management, 50*(1), 26–34.

Kennett, D. L., Durler, M. G., & Downs, A. (2007). Activity-based costing in large US cities: Costs and benefits. *Journal of Government Financial Management, 56*(1), 20.

Mohr, Z. T. (2015). An analysis of the purposes of cost accounting in large US cities. *Public Budgeting and Finance, 35*(1), 95–115.

Mohr, Z., & Mitchell, D. (2014). *Old techniques and new concepts: Cost accounting in public management networks.* Paper presented at the Western Social Sciences, Las Vegas.

Ter Bogt, H. J. (2008). Management accounting change and new public management in local government: A reassessment of ambitions and results—an institutionalist approach to accounting change in the Dutch public sector. *Financial Accountability & Management, 24*(3), 209–241.

Verbeeten, F. H. (2011). Public sector cost management practices in The Netherlands. *International Journal of Public Sector Management, 24*(6), 492–506.

Zarkin, G. A., Dunlap, L. J., & Homsi, G. (2004). The substance abuse services cost analysis program (SASCAP): A new method for estimating drug treatment services costs. *Evaluation and Program Planning, 27*(1), 35–43.

Index

Note: Italicized page numbers indicate a figure on the corresponding page. Page numbers in bold indicate a table on the corresponding page.

Printed in the United States
by Baker & Taylor Publisher Services